C000311507
S
heritage
knits

Scottish heritage knits

24 DESIGNER HANDKNITS USING ROWAN YARNS

Martin Storey

SPECIAL PHOTOGRAPHY BY JOHN HESELTINE

Scottish heritage knits
UK edition published in 2012 by
Rowan Yarns
Green Lane Mill
Holmfirth
West Yorkshire HD9 2DX

Created and produced by Berry & Bridges Ltd
Belsize Business Centre
258 Belsize Road
London NW6 4BT

Designer Anne Wilson
Editor Katie Hardwicke
Styling Susan Berry
Pattern writing and knitting Penny Hill
Technical Editor Therese Chynoweth
Charts and diagrams Therese Chynoweth
Other photography Ed Berry 15, 89, 113, 127, 145; Steven Wooster 4–5, 41, 147; Hazel Young 2–3, 7, 37, 41, 45, 51, 59, 69, 79, 93, 101, 129, 137, 152

ISBN 978-1-907544-38-5

British Library Cataloguing and Publication Data
A catalogue record of this book is available from the British Library

Reproduced and printed in Singapore

CONTENTS

Tay tartan cardigan

This richly patterned design in striking contrasting colours of 'Rowan Fine Tweed' mixes a traditional style tartan with a small snowflake motif. The tartan element used for the bottom half of the cardigan and the cuffs is knitted using the intarsia technique, while the snowflake motif for the upper front and back and sleeves is knitted in Fairisle.

FINISHED SIZE

	S	M	L	XL	
To fit bust					
	81.5–86.5	91.5–96.5	101.5–106.5	112–117	cm
	32–34	36–38	40–42	44–46	"

ACTUAL MEASUREMENTS

Bust					
	98.5	108.5	120.5	135.5	cm
	38¾	42¾	47½	53¼	"
Length to shoulder					
	52	54	56.5	58.5	cm
	20½	21¼	22¼	23	"

Sleeve length 45 cm (17¾")

YARN

'Rowan Fine Tweed' (100% wool; 90 m [98 yd]/25 g):

6 (7, 7, 8) balls in Leyburn 383 (A)
7 (7, 8, 8) balls in Pendle 377 (B)
5 (6, 6, 7) balls in Bainbridge 369 (C)
4 (4, 5, 5) balls in Malham 366 (D)

NEEDLES

Pair of 2.75 mm (U.S. size 2) knitting needles
Pair of 3.25 mm (U.S. size 3) knitting needles
Adjust needle size if necessary to obtain tension.
2.75 mm (U.S. size 2) circular needle

EXTRAS

6 buttons, 15 mm (⅝") Rowan BN1367.

TENSION

28 sts and 28 rows = 10 cm (4") in patt.

ABBREVIATIONS

See page 150.

NOTES

Read charts from right to left on RS rows and from left to right on WS rows. When working in patt, strand yarn not in use loosely across WS of work to keep fabric elastic.
When working from Chart A, use the intarsia method (see page 149).
When working from Chart B, use the Fairisle method (see page 149).

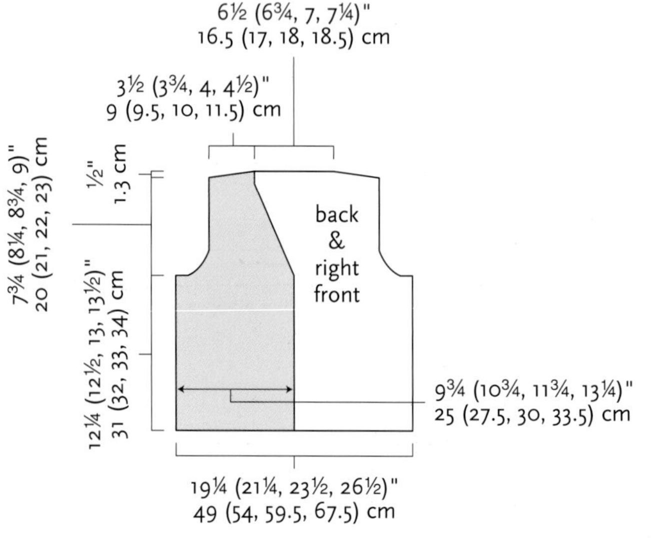

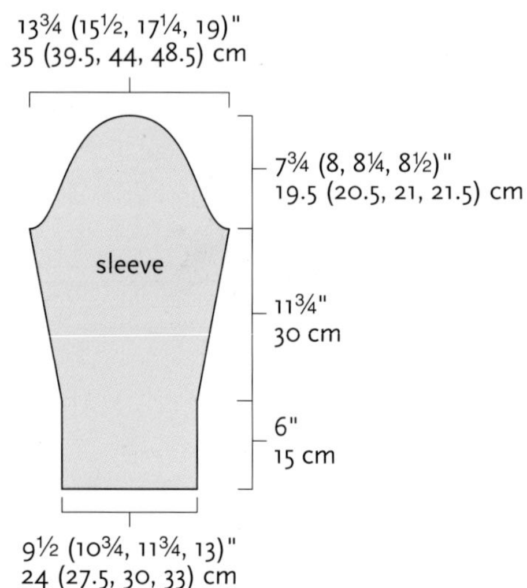

BACK

Using 2.75 mm (U.S. size 2) needles and A, cast on 135 (149, 165, 185) sts.

Knit 1 row.

Next row Work in patt from Chart A.

Cont in patt to end of Row 42.

Change to 3.25 mm (U.S. size 3) needles.

Next row Work in patt from Chart B.

Cont in patt to end of Row 27.

Rep Rows 2–27 to form patt.

Work straight until back measures 31 (32, 33, 34) cm (12¼ [12½, 13, 13½]"), ending with a WS row.

Shape armholes

Cast off 7 (9, 13, 15) sts at beg of next 2 rows – 121 (131, 139, 155) sts rem.

Dec 1 st at each end of every row 5 (7, 9, 11) times – 111 (117, 121, 133) sts rem.

Dec 1 st at each end of every RS row 8 (9, 8, 10) times – 95 (99, 105, 113) sts rem.

Work straight until back measures 51 (53, 55, 57) cm (20 [20¾, 21¾, 22½]") from cast-on edge, ending with a WS row.

Shape shoulders

Cast off 12 (13, 14, 15) sts at beg of next 2 rows, then 13 (13, 14, 16) sts at beg of foll 2 rows.

Leave the rem 45 (47, 49, 51) sts on a spare needle.

LEFT FRONT

Using 2.75 mm (U.S. size 2) needles and A, cast on 68 (75, 83, 93) sts.

Knit 1 row.

Next row Work in patt from Chart A.

Cont in patt to end of Row 42.

Change to 3.25 mm (U.S. size 3) needles.

Next row Work in patt from Chart B.

Cont in patt to end of Row 27.

Rep Rows 2–27 to form patt.

Work straight until front measures 31 (32, 33, 34) cm (12¼ [12½, 13, 13½]"), ending with a WS row.

Shape armhole and neck

Next row Cast off 7 (9, 13, 15) sts, work in patt to last 2 sts, k2tog – 60 (65, 69, 77) sts rem.

Next row Work straight in patt to end.

Next row K2tog, work in patt to last 2 sts, k2tog – 2 sts dec'd.

Next row Work in patt to last 2 sts, p2tog – 1 st dec'd.

Rep the last 2 rows 1 (2, 3, 4) more time(s), then rep the first row again – 52 (54, 55, 60) sts rem.

Next row Work straight in patt to end.

Next row K2tog, work in patt to last 2 sts, k2tog – 2 sts dec'd.

Rep the last 2 rows 7 (8, 7, 9) more times – 36 (36, 39, 40) sts rem.

Keeping armhole edge straight, cont to dec at neck edge every 4th row 11 (10, 11, 9) times – 25 (26, 28, 31) sts rem.

Work straight until front measures the same as back to shoulder, ending at armhole edge.

Shape shoulder

Next row Cast off 12 (13, 14, 15) sts, work in patt to end.

Work 1 row straight.

Cast off rem 13 (13, 14, 16) sts.

RIGHT FRONT

Using 2.75 mm (U.S. size 2) needles and A, cast on 68 (75, 83, 93) sts.

Knit 1 row.

Next row Work in patt from Chart A.

Cont in patt to end of Row 42.

Change to 3.25 mm (U.S. size 3) needles.

Next row Work in patt from Chart B.

CHART A

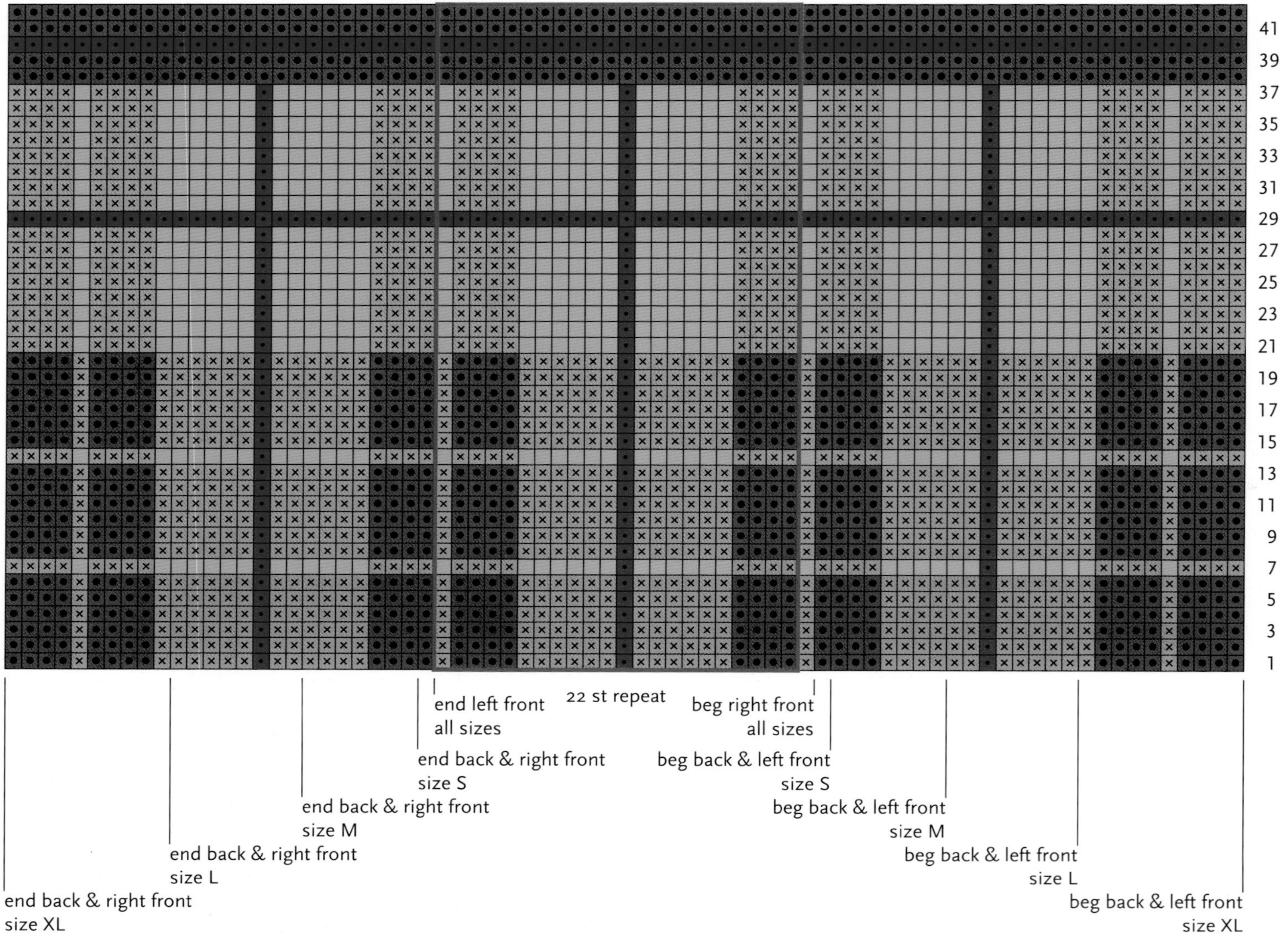

41
39
37
35
33
31
29
27
25
23
21
19
17
15
13
11
9
7
5
3
1

end left front
all sizes

22 st repeat

beg right front
all sizes

end back & right front
size S

beg back & left front
size S

end back & right front
size M

beg back & left front
size M

end back & right front
size L

beg back & left front
size L

end back & right front
size XL

beg back & left front
size XL

CHART B

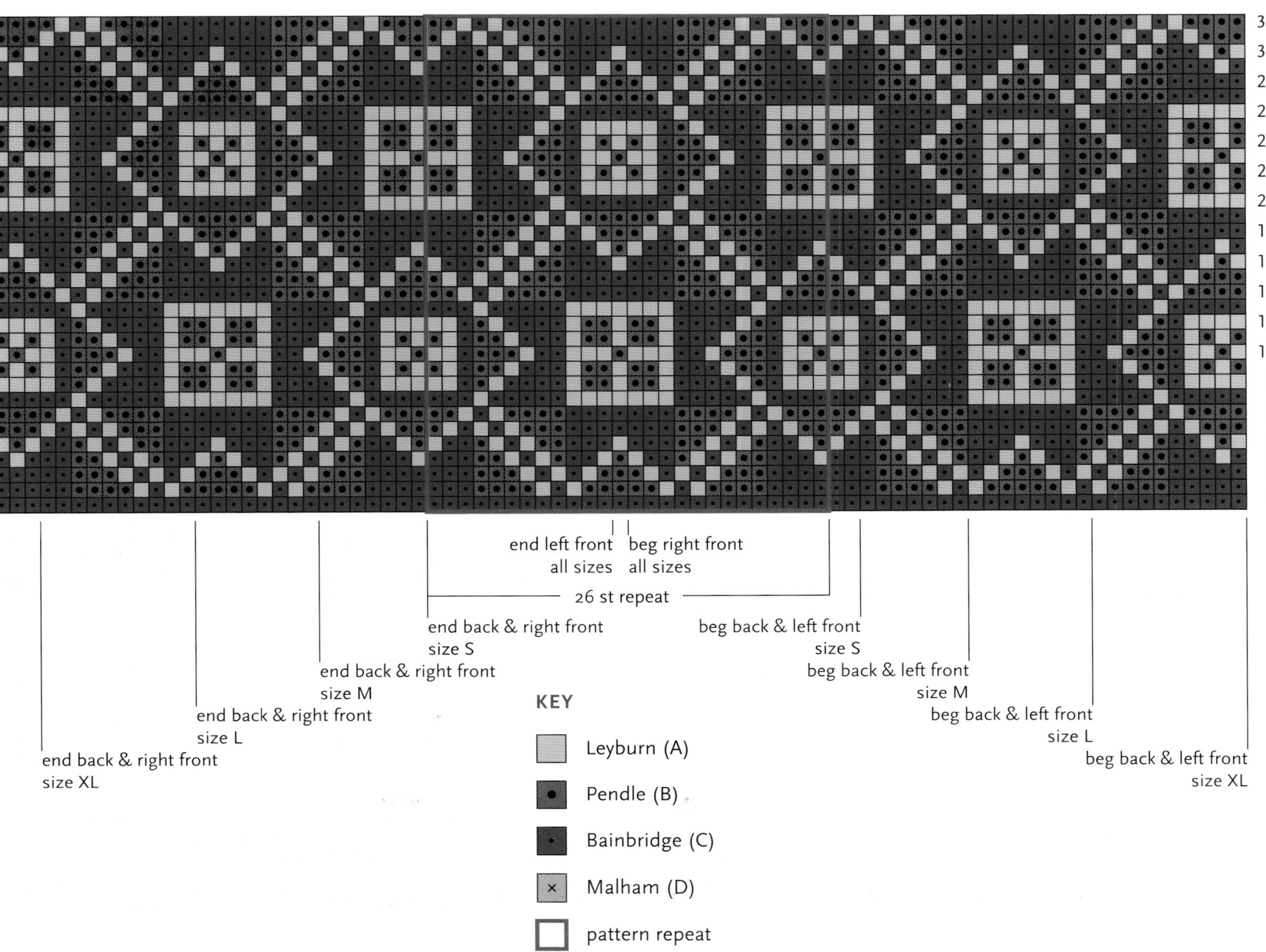
33
31
29
27
25
23
21
19
17
15
13
11
9
7
5
3
1
end left front
all sizes
beg right front
all sizes
26 st repeat
end back & right front
size S
beg back & left front
size S
end back & right front
size M
beg back & left front
size M
end back & right front
size L
beg back & left front
size L
end back & right front
size XL
beg back & left front
size XL
KEY
Leyburn (A)
Pendle (B)
Bainbridge (C)
Malham (D)
pattern repeat

Cont in patt to end of Row 27.
Rep Rows 2–27 to form patt.
Work straight until front measures 31 (32, 33, 34) cm (12¼ [12½, 13, 13½]"), ending with a WS row.

Shape armhole and neck

Next row K2tog, work in patt to end – 1 st dec'd.
Next row Cast off 7 (9, 13, 15) sts, work in patt to end – 60 (65, 69, 77) sts rem.
Next row K2tog, work in patt to last 2 sts, k2tog – 2 sts dec'd.
Next row P2tog, work in patt to end – 1 st dec'd.
Rep the last 2 rows 1 (2, 3, 4) more time(s), then rep the first row again – 52 (54, 55, 60) sts rem.
Next row Work straight in patt to end.
Next row K2tog, work in patt to last 2 sts, k2tog – 2 sts dec'd.
Rep the last 2 rows 7 (8, 7, 9) more times – 36 (36, 39, 40) sts rem.
Keeping armhole edge straight, cont to dec at neck edge every 4th row 11 (10, 11, 9) times – 25 (26, 28, 31) sts rem.
Work straight until front measures the same as back to shoulder, ending at armhole edge.

Shape shoulder

Next row Cast off 12 (13, 14, 15) sts, work in patt to end.
Work 1 row straight.
Cast off rem 13 (13, 14, 16) sts.

SLEEVES

Using 2.75 mm (U.S. size 2) needles and A, cast on 67 (75, 83, 91) sts.
Knit 1 row.
Work in patt from Chart A as foll:

Row 1 K1 (5, 9, 13) st(s) before patt rep, work across patt rep of Chart A, 3 times, work 0 (4, 8, 12) sts after patt rep.
Row 2 Work 0 (4, 8, 12) sts before patt rep, work across patt rep of Chart A, 3 times, p1 (5, 9, 13) st(s) after patt rep.
Cont in patt to end of Row 41.
Inc row P6 (8, 4, 11) [M1, p5 (4, 4, 3)] 11 (15, 19, 23) times, M1, p6 (7, 3, 11) – 79 (91, 103, 115) sts.
Change to 3.25 mm (U.S. size 3) needles.
Work in patt from Chart B as foll:
Row 1 Using C, knit to end.
Row 2 Work in patt 0 (6, 12, 5) sts before patt rep, work across patt rep of Chart B 3 (3, 3, 4) times, p1 (7, 13, 6) st(s) after patt rep.
Row 3 Work 1 (7, 13, 6) st(s) before patt rep, work across patt rep of Chart B 3 (3, 3, 4) times, 0 (6, 12, 5) sts after patt rep.
Work straight for 3 more rows.
Inc and work into patt 1 st at each end of the next row, then every 8th row 8 more times – 97 (109, 121, 133) sts.
Work straight until sleeve measures 45 cm (17¾"), ending with a row that will match back if possible.

Shape top

Cast off 7 (9, 13, 15) sts at beg of next 2 rows – 83 (91, 95, 103) sts rem.
Work 2 rows straight.
Cast off 1 (2, 3, 4) st(s) at beg of next 2 rows – 81 (87, 89, 95) sts rem.
Dec 1 st at each end of every RS row 10 times – 59 (65, 71, 77) sts rem.
Work 1 row straight.
Dec 1 st at each end of next row, then 4th row twice more – 55 (61, 63, 69) sts rem.
Dec 1 st at each end of next row, then every other row 3 more times – 47 (53, 55, 61) sts rem.
Work 1 row straight.
Dec 1 st at each end of every row 6 (8, 10, 12) times – 35 (37, 35, 37) sts rem.
Cast off 5 sts at beg on next 4 rows – 15 (17, 15, 17) sts rem.
Cast off rem sts.

FRONT BAND

Join shoulder seams.
With RS facing, using 2.75 mm (U.S. size 2) circular needle and B, pick up and k91 (93, 97, 101) sts up right front edge to beg of neck shaping, k56 (61, 64, 67) sts to shoulder, k45 (41, 45, 47) sts from back neck, pick up and k56 (61, 64, 67) sts to beg of neck shaping, then 91 (93, 97, 101) sts to cast-on edge – 339 (355, 371, 387) sts.
1st rib row P1, [k1, p1] to end.
2nd rib row K1, [p1, k1] to end.
Work 1 more row.
1st buttonhole row K1, p1, k1, p2tog, yrn, [(p1, k1) 7 times, p2tog, yrn] 5 times, work in rib to end.
Rib 4 rows straight.
Cast off loosely in rib.

MAKING UP

Join side and sleeve seams. Set in sleeves.
Sew on buttons.

Glencoe scarf

This is a relatively simple project to knit in three colours of 'Rowan Fine Tweed'. An interesting 'shadow' effect is formed as the blocks of stitches change from knit to purl, creating texture as well as pattern.

FINISHED SIZE

19 cm (7½") wide and 146 cm (57½") long

YARN

'Rowan Fine Tweed' (100% wool; 90 m [98 yd]/25 g):
3 balls in Askrigg 369 (A)
2 balls in Leyburn 383 (B)
1 ball in Richmond 381 (C)

NEEDLES

3.25 mm (U.S. size 3) needles. Adjust needle size if necessary to obtain correct tension.

TENSION

26½ sts and 42 rows = 10 cm (4") in patt.

ABBREVIATIONS

See page 150.

SCARF

With B, cast on 50 sts.
Row 1 (RS) With B, knit.
Row 2 With B, p10, [k10, p10] to end.
Row 3 With A, knit.
Row 4 With A, k10, [p10, k10] to end.
Rows 5–20 Rep Rows 1–4 four more times.
Row 21 With C, knit.
Row 22 With C, k10, [p10, k10] to end.
Row 23 With A, knit.
Row 24 With A, p10, [k10, p10] to end.
Rows 25–40 Rep Rows 21–24 four more times.
Rows 41–60 Rep Rows 1–4 five times.
Rep Rows 1–60 until piece measures 146 cm (57½"), ending with Row 58.
With B, cast off.

MAKING UP

Weave in ends. Block to finished measurements.

Tay tartan mittens

These cosy mitts employ the same mix of patterns and yarn as the Tay tartan sweater (see page 6) but in a different colourway, this time in singing blues, yellows, green and purple.

FINISHED SIZE
One size
Length 34 cm (13½")
Hand circumference 18 cm (7")

YARN
'Rowan Fine Tweed' (100% wool; 90 m [98 yd]/25 g):
1 ball each in Leyburn 383 (A), Settle 374 (B), Nidd 382 (C) and Richmond 381 (D)

NEEDLES
Pair of 3 mm (no exact U.S. equivalent; between U.S. size 2 and 3) knitting needles
Pair of 3.25 mm (U.S. size 3) knitting needles
Adjust needle size if necessary to obtain correct tension.

TENSION
28 sts and 28 rows = 10 cm (4") in chart patt using larger needles.

ABBREVIATIONS
See page 150.

MITTENS (make 2)
Using 3 mm needles and B, cast on 57 sts.
Knit 3 rows.
Beg St st and work Chart A as foll:
Row 1 (RS) K7 sts before rep, [work 22-st rep of Row 1] twice, k6 sts after rep.
Row 2 P6 sts before rep, [work 22-st rep of Row 2] twice, p7 sts after rep.
Work in established patt to end of Row 41.
Next (inc) row (WS) Using B, p1 [M1, p5] 11 times, M1, p1 – 69 sts.
Change to 3.25 mm (U.S. size 3) needles.
Work from Chart B as foll:
Row 1 (RS) Using C, knit.
Row 2 P8 sts before rep, [work 26-st rep of Row 2] twice, p9 sts after rep.
Row 3 K9 sts before rep, [work 26-st rep of Row 3] twice, k8 sts after rep.
Work 1 more row in established patt.
Next (dec) row Work 2 tog in patt, work in patt to last 2 sts, work 2 tog – 2 sts dec'd.
Work 2 rows straight.
Rep the last 3 rows 7 more times – 53 sts rem.

Thumb shaping
Row 1 (RS) Join separate strand of C, k1, M1, work in patt to last st, join separate strand of C, M1, k1 – 2 sts inc'd.
Row 2 Using C, p2, work in established patt to last 2 sts, using C, p2.
Row 3 Using C, k2, M1, work in established patt to last 2 sts, using C, M1, k2 – 2 sts inc'd.
Row 4 Using C, p3, work in established patt to last 3 sts, using C, p3.
Row 5 Using C, k3, M1, work in established

CHART A

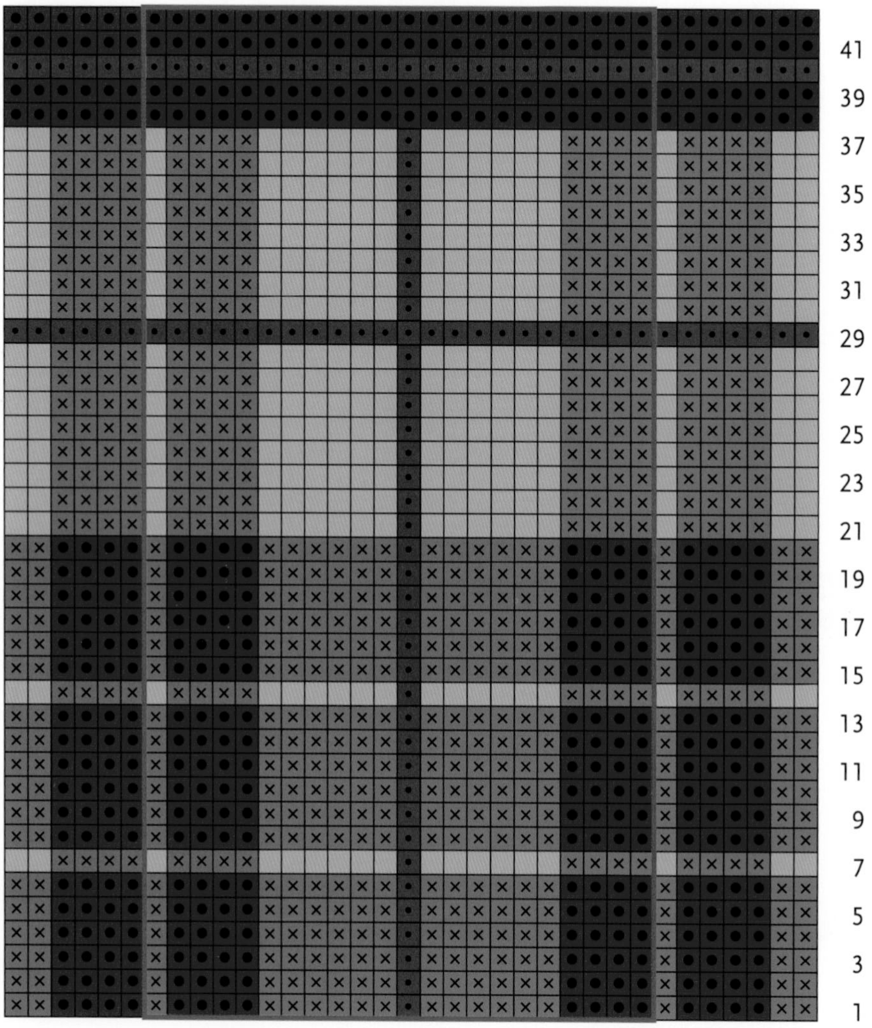

22 st repeat

KEY

- Leyburn (A)
- Settle (B)
- Nidd (C)
- Richmond (D)
- pattern repeat

NOTES

Read charts from right to left on RS rows and from left to right on WS rows. When working in patt, strand yarn not in use loosely across WS of work to keep fabric elastic.

When working from Chart A, use the intarsia method (see page 149).

When working from Chart B, use the Fairisle method (see page 149).

CHART B

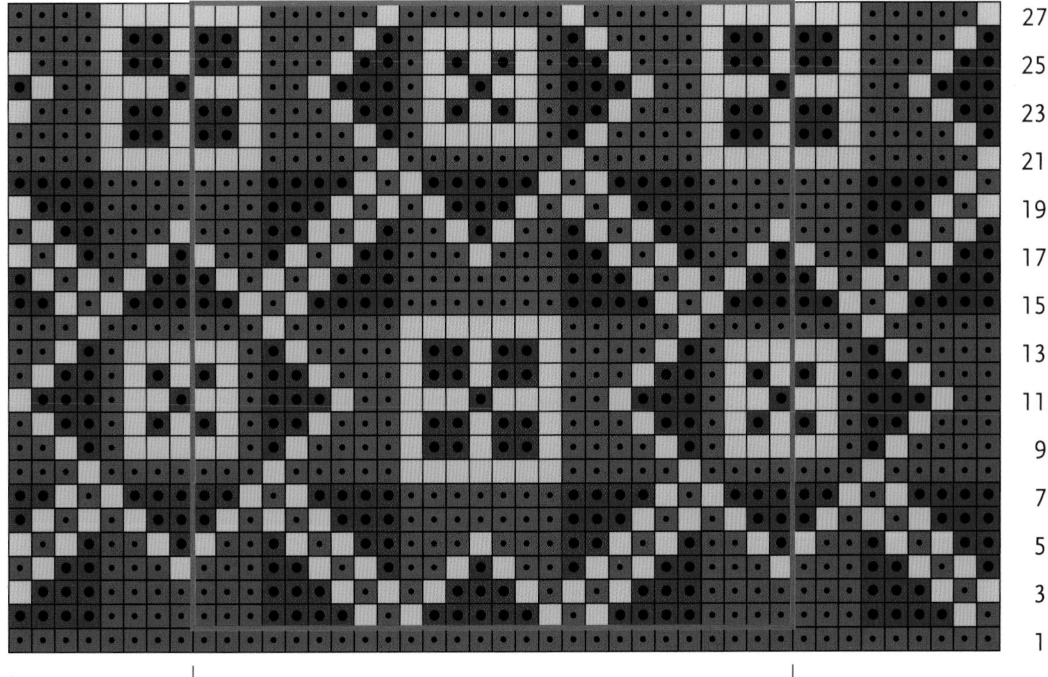

patt to last 3 sts, using C, M1, k3 – 2 sts inc'd.
Cont inc 1 st each end of every RS row 5 more times – 69 sts.

Next row (WS) Using C, p9, turn, leaving rem 60 sts unworked.

Cont in St st on these 9 sts, work 3 rows straight.

Next row (WS) Knit.

Cast off knitwise.

Return to sts on needle.

Next row (WS) Work in patt to last 9 sts, using C, p9.

Next row Using C, k9, turn, leaving rem 51 st unworked.

Cont in St st on these 9 sts, work 2 rows straight.

Next row (WS) Knit.

Cast off knitwise.

Return to sts on needle.

Next row (RS) Work in patt to end – 51 sts.

Cont in established patt, work 13 rows straight.

Change to 3 mm needles.

Using C, knit 2 rows.

Cast off knitwise.

MAKING UP

Sew side and thumb seams.

Aberdeen argyll mittens

Using the same mix of colourwork patterns as the Aberdeen argyll sweater, these mitts ring the colour changes with strong blue, green, yellow and purple. The cuffs are loose enough to wear over a jacket or jumper for extra effect.

FINISHED SIZE

One size
Length 30.5 cm (12")
Hand circumference 19.5 cm (7¾")

YARN

'Rowan Fine Tweed' (100% wool; 90 m [98 yd]/25 g):
1 ball each in Leyburn 383 (A), Bainbridge 369 (B), Richmond 381 (C), Hawes 362 (D), Burnsall 375 (E) and Hubberholme 370 (F)

NEEDLES

Pair of 3 mm (no exact U.S. equivalent; between U.S. size 2 and 3) knitting needles
Pair of 3.25 mm (U.S. size 3) knitting needles
Adjust needle size if necessary to obtain correct tension.

TENSION

25 sts and 34 rows = 10 cm (4") in Chart B patt using larger needles.

ABBREVIATIONS

See page 150.

NOTES

Read charts from right to left on RS rows and from left to right on WS rows. When working in patt, strand yarn not in use loosely across WS of work to keep fabric elastic.
When working from Chart A, use the Fairisle method (see page 149).
When working from Chart B, use the intarsia method (see page 149).

MITTENS (make 2)

Using 3 mm needles and A, cast on 69 sts.
Change to 3.25 mm (U.S. size 3) needles.
Beg St st and work Chart A as foll:
Row 1 (WS) P1 st before rep, [work 6-st rep of Row 1] 11 times, p2 sts after rep.
Row 2 K2 sts before rep, [work 6-st rep of Row 2] 11 times, k1 st after rep.
Work in established patt to end of Row 20.
Next row Using A, purl to end and dec 2 sts evenly across row – 67 sts.
Work from Chart B as foll:
Row 1 (RS) K1 st before rep, [work 16-st rep of Row 1] 4 times, k2 sts after rep.
Row 2 P2 sts before rep, [work 16-st rep of Row 2] 4 times, p1 st after rep.
Work 6 more rows in established patt.
Next (dec) row (RS) K2tog in patt, work in patt to last 2 sts, k2tog – 2 sts dec'd.
Work 5 rows straight.
Rep the last 6 rows 6 more times – 53 sts rem.

Thumb shaping

Row 1 (RS) Join separate strand of C, k1, M1, work in established patt to last st, join separate strand of C, M1, k1 – 2 sts inc'd.
Row 2 Using C, p2, work in established patt to last 2 sts, using C, p2.
Row 3 Using C, k2, M1, work in established patt to last 2 sts, using C, M1, k2 – 2 sts inc'd.
Row 4 Using C, p3, work in established patt to last 3 sts, using C, p3.
Row 5 Using C, k3, M1, work in established patt to last 3 sts, using C, M1, k3 – 2 sts inc'd.
Cont inc 1 st each end of every RS row 5 more times – 69 sts.
Next row (WS) Using C, p9, turn, leaving rem 60 sts unworked.
Cont in St st on these 9 sts, work 3 rows straight.
Next row (WS) Knit.
Cast off knitwise.
Return to sts on needle.
Next row (WS) Work in patt to last 9 sts, using C, p9.
Next row Using C, k9, turn, leaving rem 51 sts unworked.
Cont in St st on these 9 sts, work 2 rows straight.
Next row (WS) Knit.
Cast off knitwise.
Return to sts on needle.
Next row (RS) Work in patt to end – 51 sts.
Cont in established patt, work 15 rows straight.
Change to 3 mm needles.
Using E, knit 2 rows.
Cast off knitwise.

MAKING UP

Sew side and thumb seams.

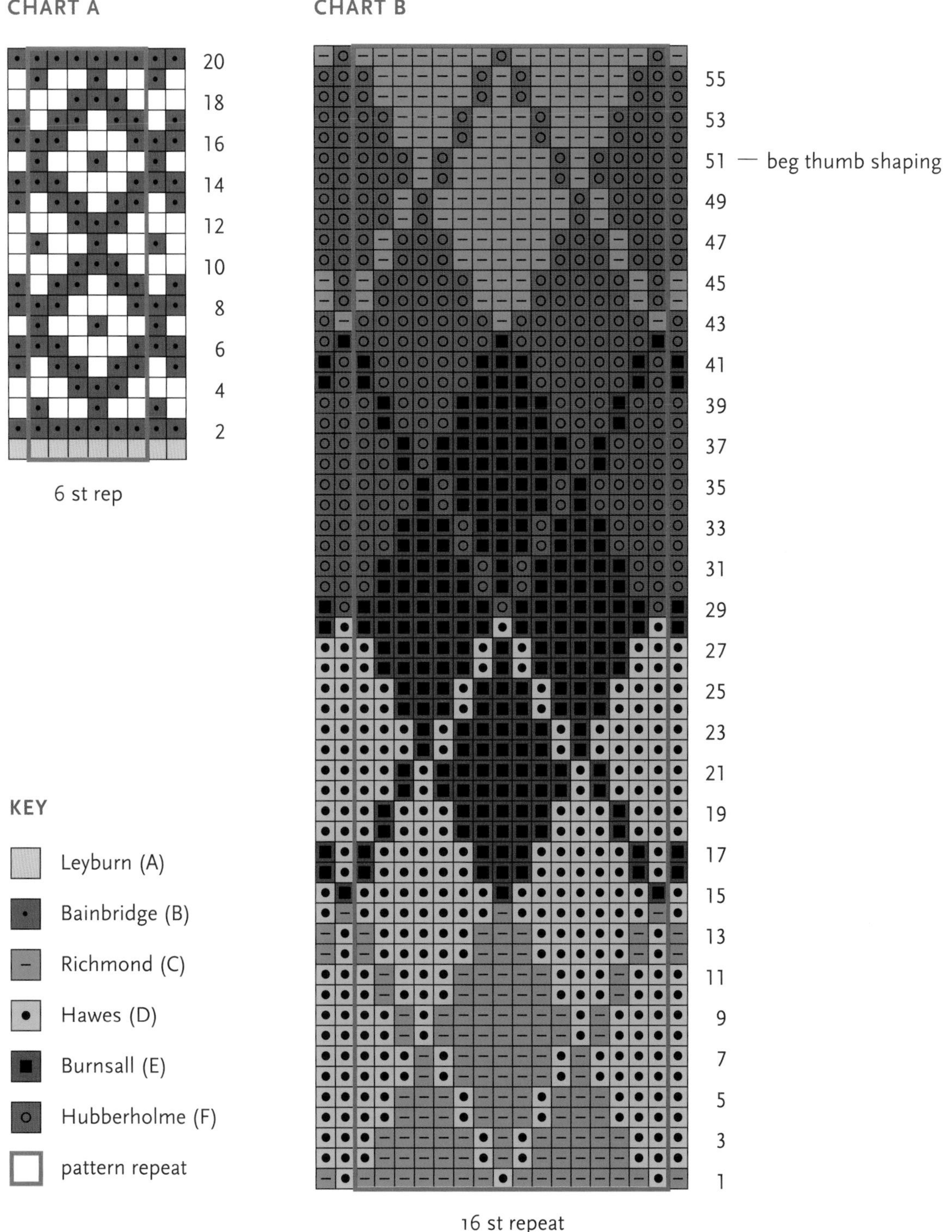
CHART A
20
18
16
14
12
10
8
6
4
2
6 st rep
CHART B
55
53
51 — beg thumb shaping
49
47
45
43
41
39
37
35
33
31
29
27
25
23
21
19
17
15
13
11
9
7
5
3
1
16 st repeat
KEY
Leyburn (A)
Bainbridge (B)
Richmond (C)
Hawes (D)
Burnsall (E)
Hubberholme (F)
pattern repeat

Aberdeen argyll sweater

A really clever mix of contrasting patterns and strong singing colours. A knock-out colourwork number, it has a simple but flattering shape with its slightly shorter length and lowered round neckline. Knitted in a finer yarn, 'Rowan Fine Tweed', it is warm but stays flexible.

FINISHED SIZE

	S	M	L	XL	
To fit bust					
	81.5–86.5	91.5–96.5	101.5–106.5	112–117	cm
	32–34	36–38	40–42	44–46	"

ACTUAL MEASUREMENTS

	S	M	L	XL	
Bust					
	101	113	125.5	138.5	cm
	39¾	44½	49½	54½	"
Length to shoulder					
	52	54	56.5	58.5	cm
	20½	21¼	22¼	23	"

Sleeve length 45 cm (17¾")

YARN

'Rowan Fine Tweed' (100% wool; 90 m [98 yd]/25 g):

1 (1, 2, 2) ball(s) each in Leyburn 383 (A) and Bainbridge 369 (B)

4 (4, 5, 5) balls each in Richmond 381 (C), Hawes 362 (D), Burnsall 375 (E) and Hubberholme 370 (F)

NEEDLES

Pair of 3 mm (no exact U.S. equivalent; between U.S. size 2 and 3) knitting needles

Pair of 3.25 mm (U.S. size 3) knitting needles

Adjust needle size if necessary to obtain correct tension.

EXTRAS

Stitch holders.

TENSION

26 sts and 34 rows = 10 cm (4") in Chart B patt using 3.25 mm (U.S. size 3) needles.

ABBREVIATIONS

See page 150.

NOTES

Read Charts from right to left on RS rows and from left to right on WS rows. When working in patt, strand yarn not in use loosely across WS of work to keep fabric elastic.

When working from Chart A, use the Fairisle method (see page 149).

When working from Chart B, use the intarsia method (see page 149).

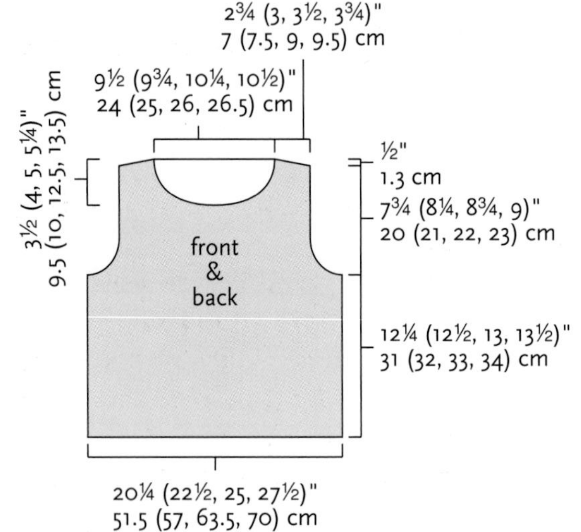

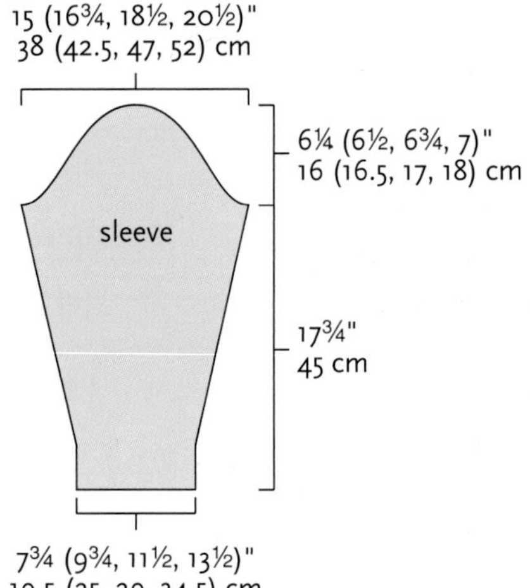

BACK

Using 3 mm needles and A, cast on 131 (147, 163, 179) sts.
Change to 3.25 mm (U.S. size 3) needles.
Beg St st and work Chart A as foll:
Row 1 (WS) P2 (1, 0, 2) st(s) before rep, [work 6-st rep of Row 1] 21 (24, 27, 29) times, p3 (2, 1, 3) st(s) after rep.
Row 2 K3 (2, 1, 3) st(s) before rep, [work 6-st rep of Row 2] 21 (24, 27, 29) times, k2 (1, 0, 2) st(s) after rep.
Cont in established patt to end of Row 21.
Work Chart B as foll:
Row 1 (RS) K1 st before rep, [work 16-st rep of Row 1] 8 (9, 10, 11) times, k2 sts after rep.
Row 2 P2 sts before rep, [work 16-st rep of Row 2] 8 (9, 10, 11) times, p1 st after rep.
Cont in established patt until back measures 31 (32, 33, 34) cm (12¼ [12½, 13, 13½]") from cast on, ending with a WS row.

Shape armholes

Cast off 8 (9, 10, 11) sts at beg of next 2 rows – 115 (129, 143, 157) sts rem.
Cast off 2 (2, 3, 3) sts at beg of next 4 (12, 4, 12) rows, then 1 (1, 2, 2) st(s) at beg of next 10 (2, 10, 2) rows – 97 (103, 111, 117) sts rem.
Work straight until piece measures 51 (53, 55, 57) cm (20 [20¾, 21¾, 22½]") from cast on, ending with a WS row.

Shape shoulders

Cast off 9 (10, 11, 12) sts at beg of next 4 rows – 61 (63, 67, 69) sts rem.
Leave the rem sts on a spare needle.

FRONT

Work as given for back until front measures 43 (44, 44, 45) cm (17 [17¼, 17¼, 17¾]") from cast on, ending with a WS row.

Shape neck

Next row (RS) K36 (38, 40, 42), turn, leaving rem 61 (65, 71, 75) sts on holder.
Next row Cast off 2 sts, work in patt to end.
Next row Work in patt to last 2 sts, k2tog – 1 st dec'd.
Rep the last 2 rows 5 more times – 18 (20, 22, 24) sts rem.
Work straight until front measures the same as back to shoulder, ending at armhole edge with a WS row.

Shape left shoulder

Cast off 9 (10, 11, 12) at the beg of next 2 RS rows.
With RS facing, place next 25 (27, 31, 33) sts on a holder, rejoin yarn to rem 36 (38, 40, 42) sts, work in patt to end.
Next row Work in patt to last 2 sts, p2tog tbl – 1 st dec'd.
Next row Cast off 2 sts, work in patt to end.
Rep the last 2 rows 5 more times – 18 (20, 22, 24) sts rem.
Work straight until front measures the same as back to shoulder, ending at armhole edge with a RS row.

Shape right shoulder

Cast off 9 (10, 11, 12) sts at beg of next 2 WS rows.

SLEEVES

Using 3 mm needles and A, cast on 51 (63, 75, 87) sts.
Change to 3.25 mm (U.S. size 3) needles.
Beg St st and work Chart A as foll:
Row 1 (WS) P1 st before rep, [work 16-st rep of Row 1] 8 (10, 12, 14) times, p2 sts after rep.
Row 2 K2 sts before rep, [work 16-st rep of Row 2] 8 (10, 12, 14) times, k1 st after rep.
Cont in established patt to end of Row 21.

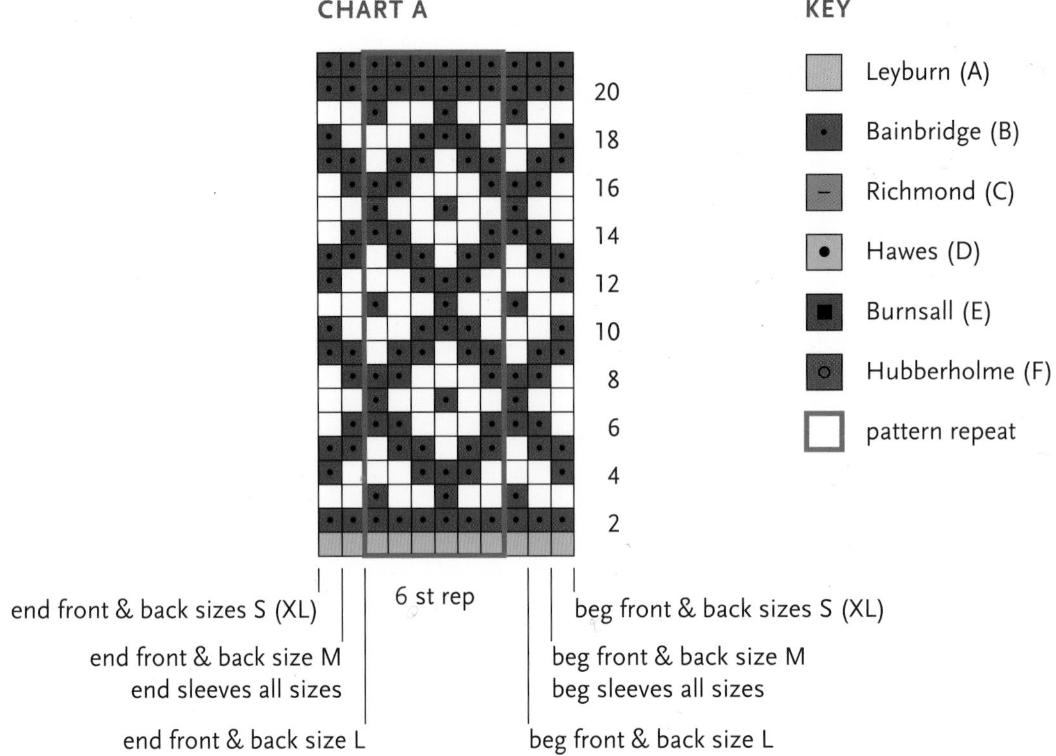

Work Chart B as foll:

Row 1 (RS) K1 (7, 4, 3) st(s) before rep, [work 16-st rep of Row 1] 3 (3, 4, 5) times, k2 (8, 5, 4) sts after rep.

Row 2 P2 (8, 5, 4) sts before rep, [work 16-st rep of Row 2] 3 (3, 4, 5) times, p1 (7, 4, 3) st(s) after rep.

Cont in established patt and AT THE SAME TIME, inc 1 st at each end of the next row, every 4 rows 6 times, then every 6 rows 16 times – 97 (109, 121, 133) sts. Work new sts in patt.

Work straight until sleeve measures 45 cm (17¾") from cast on, ending with a WS row.

Shape top

Cast off 8 (10, 12, 14) sts at beg of next 2 rows – 81 (89, 97, 105) sts rem.

Work 2 rows straight.

Cast off 1 (2, 3, 4) st(s) at beg of next 2 rows – 79 (85, 91, 97) sts rem.

Dec 1 st at each end of every RS row 10 times – 59 (65, 71, 77) sts rem.

Work 1 row straight.

Dec 1 st at each end of next row, then every 4 rows 2 times – 53 (59, 65, 71) sts rem.

Work 1 row straight.

Dec 1 st at each end of every RS row 4 times – 45 (51, 57, 63) sts rem.

CHART B

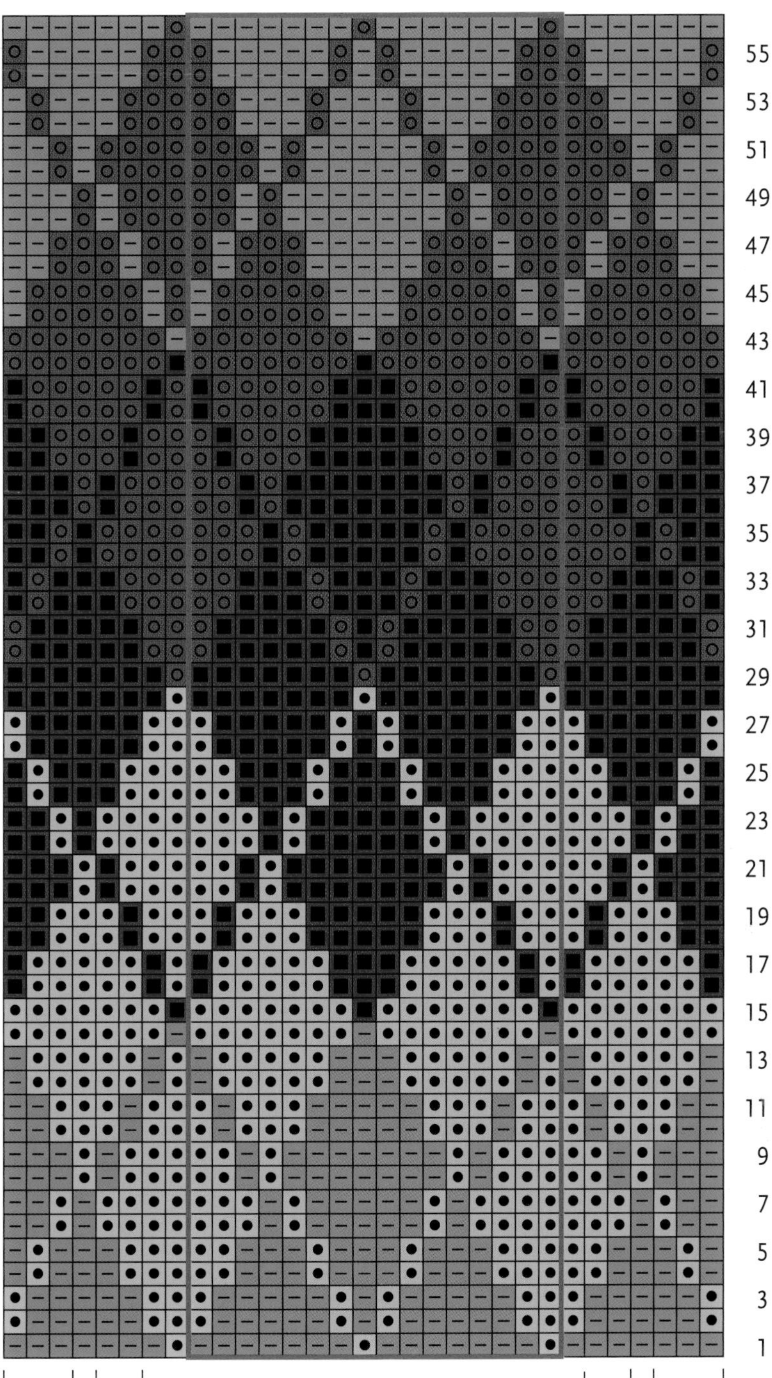

55
53
51
49
47
45
43
41
39
37
35
33
31
29
27
25
23
21
19
17
15
13
11
9
7
5
3
1
16 st repeat
end sleeve size M
beg sleeve size L
beg sleeve size XL
end front & back all sizes
end sleeve size S
beg sleeve size M
beg sleeve size L
beg sleeve size XL
beg front & back all sizes
beg sleeve size S

Work 1 row straight.
Dec 1 st at each end of every row 5 (7, 9, 11) times – 35 (37, 39, 41) sts rem.
Cast off 5 sts at beg on next 4 rows – 15 (17, 19, 21) sts rem.
Cast off rem sts.

MAKING UP

Weave in ends. Block to finished measurements.

Neckband

Sew right shoulder seam.
With RS facing, using 3 mm needles and C, pick up and k30 (30, 32, 32) sts along left front neck, k25 (27, 31, 33) sts from front neck holder, pick up and k30 (30, 32, 32) sts along right front neck, k61 (63, 67, 69) sts from back neck holder – 146 (150, 162, 166) sts.
Rib row [K1, p1] to end.
Rep the last row 6 more times.
Cast off in rib.
Sew left shoulder and neckband seam.
Sew side and sleeve seams.
Sew in sleeves.

Shetland cushion

This cushion in Rowan 'Felted Tweed DK', a soft mixture of merino wool and alpaca, with a little viscose, has beautifully subtle blends of colour, just like the traditional dyes of Shetland wool. It is designed in separate blocks, knitted using the Fairisle technique. They are sewn together at the end, like patchwork.

FINISHED SIZE
38 x 38 cm (15 x 15")

YARN
Rowan 'Felted Tweed DK' (50% merino wool, 25% alpaca, 25% viscose; 175 m [191 yd]/50 g):
1 ball each in Camel 157 (A1), Avocado 161 (A2), Cinnamon 175 (B1), Rage 150 (B2), Seafarer 170 (C1), Paisley 171 (C2), Duck Egg 173 (D1) and Treacle 145 (D2)

NEEDLES
Pair of 3.75 mm (U.S. size 5) knitting needles
Adjust needle size if necessary to obtain correct tension.

EXTRAS
Cushion pad, 40.5 cm (16") square

TENSION
Each block measures 19 cm (7½") square.

ABBREVIATIONS
See page 150.

NOTES
Read charts from right to left on RS rows and from left to right on WS rows. When working in patt, strand yarn not in use loosely across WS of work to keep fabric elastic.
When working from charts, use the Fairisle method (see page 149).

BLOCK A (make 4)
Using 3.75 mm (U.S. size 5) needles and Camel (A1), cast on 53 sts.
Work in patt from chart using key A.
Cast off.

BLOCK B (make 4)
Using 3.75 mm (U.S. size 5) needles and Avocado (A2), cast on 53 sts.
Work in patt from chart using key B.
Cast off.

MAKING UP
Sew 4 blocks together, alternating blocks A and B to form a square, 2 blocks wide by 2 blocks long.
Make second square to match. Sew squares together along 3 sides. Insert cushion pad, then sew together along 4th side.

53 sts

KEY A

- Camel (A1)
- ○ Cinnamon (B1)
- • Seafarer (C1)
- × Duck Egg (D1)

KEY B

- Avocado (A2)
- ○ Rage (B2)
- • Paisley (C2)
- × Treacle (D2)

ASSEMBLY DIAGRAM

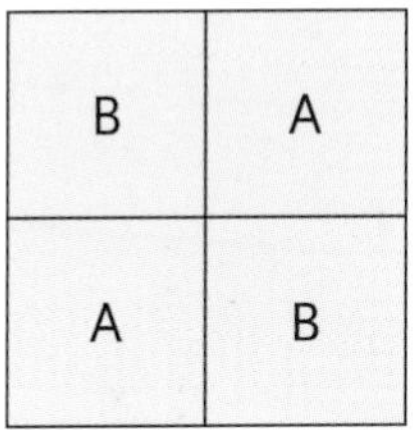

B	A
A	B

Shetland knee rug and throw

This lovely, softly toned throw is made from patched squares of two alternating colourways in the same design and yarns as the Shetland cushion (see page 36). You can make it as big or small as you like: the small size is ideal as a knee rug or chair back throw. The larger size makes a good bed cover.

FINISHED SIZE

Knee rug: 95 x 95 cm (37½ x 37½")
Throw: 133 cm (52¼") wide x 171 cm (67¼") long

YARN

Rowan 'Felted Tweed DK' (50% merino wool, 25% alpaca, 25% viscose; 175 m [191 yd]/50 g):

Knee rug

3 balls each in Camel 157 (A1) and Avocado 161 (A2)
1 ball each in Cinnamon 175 (B1), Rage 150 (B2), Seafarer 170 (C1), Paisley 171 (C2), Duck Egg 173 (D1) and Treacle 145 (D2)

Throw

7 balls each in Camel 157 (A1) and Avocado 161 (A2)
2 balls each in Cinnamon 175 (B1), Rage 150 (B2), Seafarer 170 (C1), Paisley 171 (C2), Duck Egg 173 (D1) and Treacle 145 (D2)

NEEDLES

Pair of 3.75 mm (U.S. size 5) knitting needles
Adjust needle size if necessary to obtain correct tension.

TENSION

Each block measures 19 cm (7½") square.

ABBREVIATIONS

See page 150.

NOTES

See chart on page 39. Read chart from right to left on RS rows and from left to right on WS rows. When working in patt, strand yarn not in use loosely across WS of work to keep fabric elastic.
When working from chart, use the Fairisle method (see page 149).

BLOCK A (make 12 [31])

Using 3.75 mm (U.S size 5) needles and Camel (A1), cast on 53 sts.
Work in patt from Chart on page 39 using Key A.
Cast off.

BLOCK B (make 13 [32])

Using 3.75 mm (U.S size 5) needles and Avocado (A2), cast on 53 sts.
Work in patt from Chart on page 39 using Key B.
Cast off.

MAKING UP

With a Block B in each corner, sew blocks together alternating Blocks A and B to form a square 5 blocks wide by 5 blocks long, or a rectangle 7 blocks wide by 9 blocks long, using diagram below as guide.

ASSEMBLY DIAGRAM

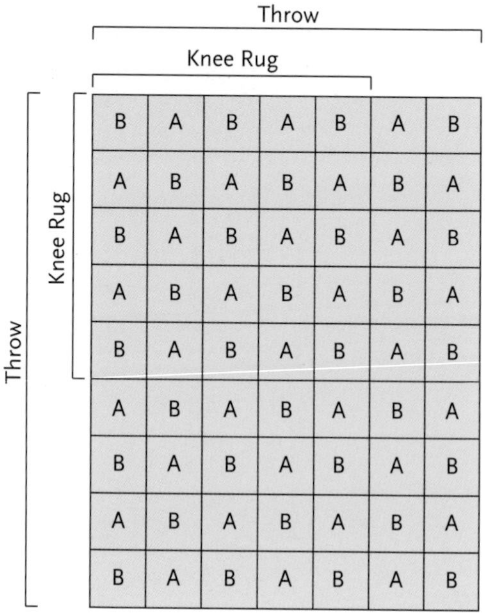

Throw

Knee Rug

B	A	B	A	B	A	B
A	B	A	B	A	B	A
B	A	B	A	B	A	B
A	B	A	B	A	B	A
B	A	B	A	B	A	B
A	B	A	B	A	B	A
B	A	B	A	B	A	B
A	B	A	B	A	B	A
B	A	B	A	B	A	B

Knee Rug

Throw

Skye poncho

This cosy, outsize cover-up is knitted in 'Rowan Tweed Aran', which speeds up the knitting and also adds extra warmth. Just the thing for crisp winter days in the countryside.

FINISHED SIZE
138.5 cm (54½") width, including trim and 68 cm (26¾") long, including trim

YARN
28 balls of Rowan 'Tweed Aran' (50% merino wool, 25% alpaca, 25% viscose; 175 m [191 yd]/50 g) in Malham 774

NEEDLES
Pair of 4 mm (U.S. size 6) knitting needles
4.5 mm (U.S. size 7) needles: one pair straight needles and 100 cm (40") long circular (cir) needle
Adjust needle size if necessary to obtain correct tension.
Cable needle (cn)

TENSION
17 sts and 26 rows = 10 cm (4") in St st using 4.5 mm (U.S. size 7) needles.

ABBREVIATIONS
C6B: slip next 3 sts onto cn and hold in back of work, k3, then k3 from cn.
C6F: slip next 3 sts onto cn and hold in front of work, k3, then k3 from cn.
C9B: slip next 4 sts onto cn and hold in back of work, k5, then k4 from cn.
C4R: slip next st onto cn and hold in back of work, k3, then k1 from cn.
C4L: slip next 3 sts onto cn and hold in front of work, k1, then k3 from cn.
T4R: slip next 2 sts onto cn and hold in back of work, k2, then p2 from cn.
T4L: slip next 2 sts onto cn and hold in front of work, p2, then k2 from cn.
See also page 150.

PATT PANEL A (20 sts)
Row 1 (RS) P8, [k2, p2] 3 times.
Row 2 [K2, p2] 3 times, k8.
Row 3 P6, [T4R] 3 times, p2.
Row 4 K4, [p2, k2] twice, p2, k6.
Row 5 P4, [T4R] 3 times, p4.
Row 6 K6, [p2, k2] twice, p2, k4.
Row 7 P2, [T4R] 3 times, p6.
Row 8 K8, [p2, k2] 3 times.
Row 9 [P2, k2] 3 times, p8.
Row 10 Rep Row 8.
Row 11 P2, [T4L] 3 times, p6.
Row 12 Rep Row 6.
Row 13 P4, [T4L] 3 times, p4.
Row 14 Rep Row 4.
Row 15 P6, [T4L] 3 times, p2.
Row 16 Rep Row 2.
Rep Rows 1–16 for patt.

PATT PANEL B (12 sts)
Row 1 (RS) K1, p2, k6, p2, k1.
Row 2 P1, k2, p6, k2, p1.
Row 3 K1, p2, C6F, p2, k1.
Row 4 Rep Row 2.
Row 5 Rep Row 1.
Row 6 Rep Row 2.
Rep Rows 1–6 for patt.

PATT PANEL C (42 sts)
Row 1 (RS) [P2, k3] 3 times, p3, C6F, p3, [k3, p2] 3 times.
Row 2 [K2, p3] 3 times, k3, p6, k3, [p3, k2] 3 times.
Row 3 [P2, k3] 3 times, p2, C4R, C4L, p2, [k3, p2] 3 times.
Row 4 [K2, p3] 3 times, k2, [p3, k2] 5 times.
Row 5 [P2, k3] 8 times.
Row 6 [K2, p3] 8 times.
Row 7 [P2, k3] 3 times, p2, C4L, C4R, p2, [k3, p2] 3 times.
Row 8 [K2, p3] 3 times, k3, p6, k3, [p3, k2] 3 times.
Row 9 [P2, k3] twice, p2, C4L, p2, C6F, p2,

C4R, p2, [k3, p2] twice.
Row 10 [K2, p3] twice, k3, p3, k2, p6, k2, p3, k3, [p3, k2] twice.
Row 11 P2, k3, [p2, C4L] twice, C4R, C4L, [C4R, p2] twice, k3, p2.
Row 12 K2, [p3, k3] twice, p6, k2, p6, [k3, p3] twice, k2.
Row 13 P2, [C4L, p2] twice, [C6B, p2] twice [C4R, p2] twice.
Row 14 [K3, p3] twice, [k2, p6] twice, k2, [p3, k3] twice.
Row 15 P3, C4L, p2, [C4L, C4R] 3 times, p2, C4R, p3.
Row 16 K4, p3, k3, [p6, k2] twice, p6, k3, p3, k4.
Row 17 P4, C4L, [p2, C6F] 3 times, p2, C4R, p4.
Row 18 K5, p3, k2, [p6, k2] 3 times, p3, k5.
Row 19 P5, [C4L, C4R] 4 times, p5.
Row 20 K6, [p6, k2] 3 times, p6, k6.
Row 21 P6, [C6F, p2] 3 times, C6B, p6.
Row 22 Rep Row 20.
Row 23 P5, [C4R, C4L] 4 times, p5.
Row 24 Rep Row 18.
Row 25 P5, k3, p2, [C6F, p2] 3 times, k3, p5.
Row 26 Rep Row 18.
Row 27 P5, [C4L, C4R] 4 times, p5.
Row 28 Rep Row 20.
Row 29 Rep Row 21.
Row 30 Rep Row 20.
Row 31 Rep Row 23.
Row 32 Rep Row 18.
Row 33 P4, C4R, [p2, C6F] 3 times, p2, C4L, p4.
Row 34 Rep Row 16.
Row 35 P3, C4R, p2, [C4R, C4L] 3 times, p2, C4L, p3.
Row 36 Rep Row 14.
Row 37 P2, [C4R, p2] twice, [C6B, p2] twice, [C4L, p2] twice.
Row 38 Rep Row 12.
Row 39 P2, k3, [p2, C4R] twice, C4L, C4R, [C4L, p2] twice, k3, p2.
Row 40 Rep Row 10.
Row 41 [P2, k3] twice, p2, C4R, p2, C6F, p2, C4L, p2, [k3, p2] twice.
Row 42 Rep Row 8.
Rows 43–48 Rep Rows 3–8.
Rep Rows 1–48 for patt.

PATT PANEL D (20 sts)
Row 1 (RS) [P2, k2] 3 times, p8.
Row 2 K8, [p2, k2] 3 times.
Row 3 P2, [T4L] 3 times, p6.
Row 4 K6, [p2, k2] twice, p2, k4.
Row 5 P4, [T4L] 3 times, p4.
Row 6 K4, [p2, k2] twice, p2, k6.
Row 7 P6, [T4L] 3 times, p2.
Row 8 [K2, p2] 3 times, k8.
Row 9 P8, [k2, p2] 3 times.
Row 10 Rep Row 8.
Row 11 P6, [T4R] 3 times, p2.
Row 12 Rep Row 6.
Row 13 P4, [T4R] 3 times, p4.
Row 14 Rep Row 4.
Row 15 P2, [T4R] 3 times, p6.
Row 16 Rep Row 2.
Rep Rows 1–16 for patt.

BACK
Using 4.5 mm (U.S. size 7) cir needle, cast on 260 sts.
Foundation row (WS) K85, [p2, k2] 3 times, p1, k2, [p2, k2] twice, p1, [k2, p3] 8 times, k2, p1, k2, [p2, k2] twice, p1, [k2, p2] 3 times, k85.
Row 1 K77, work across Row 1 of Panels A, B, C, B, then D, k77.
Row 2 P77, work across Row 2 of Panels D, B, C, B, then A, p77.
Keeping 77 sts at each side in St st, work in established patt until piece measures 64 cm (25¼") from cast on, ending with a WS row.

Cast off 101 sts at beg of next 2 rows – 58 sts. Cast off rem sts and dec 8 sts over Panel C and 2 sts over each Panel B.

FRONT

Work same as Back until piece measures 56 cm (22") from cast on, ending with a WS row.

Front neck shaping

Next row Work 111 sts, turn, leaving rem 149 sts on hold.

Next row Cast off 2 sts, work in patt to end – 109 sts rem.

Work 1 WS row straight.

Rep the last 2 rows 4 more times – 101 sts rem.

Work straight until front measures the same as back, ending at side edge.

Cast off rem sts.

With RS facing, rejoin yarn to rem sts, cast off next 38 sts and dec 8 sts evenly across, work in patt to end – 111 sts rem.

Work 1 WS row straight.

Next row Cast off 2 sts, work in patt to end – 109 sts rem.

Work 1 WS row straight.

Rep the last 2 rows 4 more times – 101 sts rem.

Work straight until front measures the same as back, ending at side edge.

Cast off rem sts.

COLLAR

Sew shoulder seams.

Using 4.5 mm (U.S. size 7) needles, cast on 22 sts.

Row 1 (RS) P2, knit to last 2 sts, p2.

Row 2 Purl.

Row 3 P2 [C6B] 3 times, p2.

Row 4 Purl.

Rows 5 and 6 Rep Rows 1 and 2.

Row 7 P2, k3, [C6F] twice, k3, p2.

Row 8 Purl.

Rep Rows 1–8 until collar fits round neck edge. Cast off in patt.

CABLE TRIM

Using 4 mm (U.S. size 6) needles, cast on 11 sts.

Row 1 (RS) P2, k9.

Row 2 P9, k2.

Row 3 and 4 Rep Rows 1 and 2.

Row 5 P2, C9B.

Row 6 Rep Row 2.

Rows 7–12 Rep Rows 1 and 2, three times.

Rep Rows 1–12 until trim fits around entire outer edge of poncho.

Cast off in patt.

MAKING UP

Sew cast-on and cast-off edges of collar together. Sew collar to neck edge. Sew cast-on and cast-off edges of cable trim. Placing cable edge at outer edge, gathering edging at corners so it remains flat, sew in place.

Mackintosh rose jacket

This bolero-style jacket with three-quarter sleeves is knitted in 'Rowan Fine Tweed' in elegant grey and black. The lightly frilled lacy edging to the hem and sleeves gives it extra feminine appeal.

FINISHED SIZE

	S	M	L	XL	
To fit bust					
	81.5–86.5	91.5–96.5	101.5–106.5	112–117	cm
	32–34	36–38	40–42	44–46	"

ACTUAL MEASUREMENTS

Bust					
	91.5	102	113	124.5	cm
	36	40¼	44½	49	"
Length to shoulder					
	53.5	54	55	56.5	cm
	21	21¼	21¾	22¼	"

Sleeve length 33 cm (13")

YARN

'Rowan Fine Tweed' (100% wool; 90 m [98 yd]/25 g):
9 (10, 11, 12) balls in Buckden 364 (A)
4 (5, 5, 6) balls in Malham 366 (B)
4 (4, 5, 5) balls in Pendle 377 (C)

NEEDLES

Pair of 3 mm (no exact U.S. equivalent; between U.S. size 2 and 3) knitting needles
Pair of 3.25 mm (U.S. size 3) knitting needles
Adjust needle size if necessary to obtain correct tension.

TENSION

30 sts and 34 rows = 10 cm (4") in colour patt using larger needles.

ABBREVIATIONS

MB: make bobble, [k1, yf, k1] in next st, turn, p3, turn, k3, turn, p3, sk2p, to complete bobble – 1 st rem.
See also page 150.

NOTES

Read charts from right to left on RS rows and from left to right on WS rows. When working in patt, strand yarn not in use loosely across WS of work to keep fabric elastic.
When working from chart, use the intarsia method (see page 149).

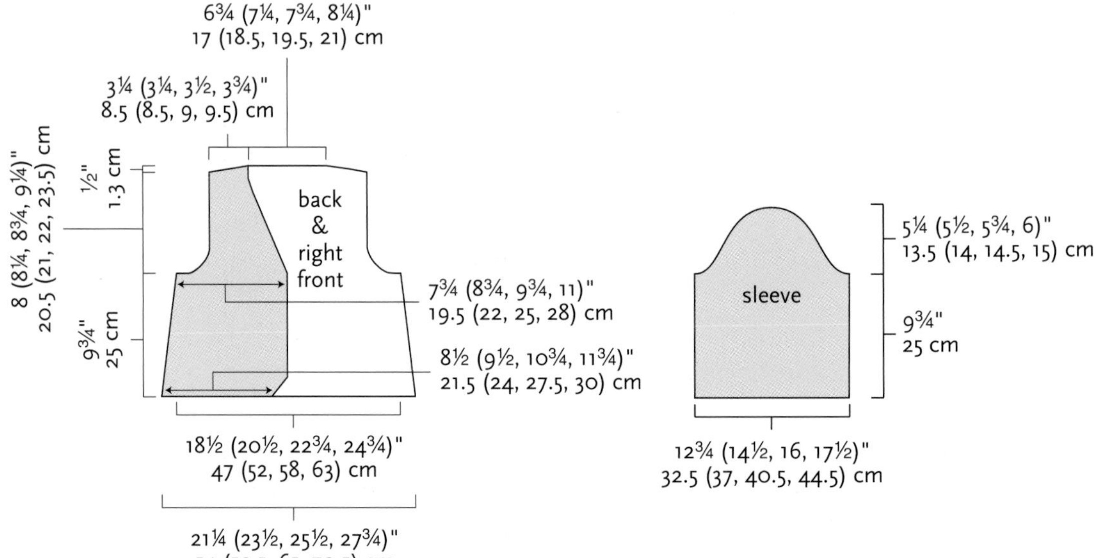

BACK

Using 3.25 mm (U.S. size 3) needles and A, cast on 160 (176, 192, 208) sts.

Purl 1 row.

Work in patt from Chart as foll:

Row 1 Ko (8, 16, 4) sts before rep, work 40-st rep of Row 1 four (four, four, five) times, ko (8, 16, 4) sts after rep.

Row 2 Po (8, 16, 4) sts before rep, work 40-st rep of Row 2 four (four, four, five) times, po (8, 16, 4) sts after rep.

Work in established patt for 4 more rows.

Dec 1 st at each end of next row – 2 sts dec'd.

Work 5 rows straight.

Rep the last 6 rows 9 more times, then rep the dec row once more – 138 (154, 170, 186) sts rem.

Work straight until back measures 25 cm (9¾") from cast-on edge, ending with a WS row.

Shape armholes

Cast off 7 (9, 11, 13) sts at beg of next 2 rows – 124 (136, 148, 160) sts rem.

Dec 1 st at each end of the next 5 (7, 9, 11) rows then every RS row 16 (18, 18, 20) times – 98 (104, 112, 118) sts rem.

Work straight until armhole measures 20.5 (21, 22, 23.5) cm (8 [8¼, 8¾, 9¼]"), ending with a WS row.

Shape shoulders

Cast off 12 (12, 13, 14) sts at beg of next 2 rows, then 12 (13, 14, 14) sts at beg of next 2 rows – 50 (54, 58, 62) sts rem.

Cast off rem sts.

LEFT FRONT

Using 3.25 mm (U.S. size 3) needles and A, cast on 64 (72, 80, 88) sts.

Purl 1 row.

Work in patt from Chart as foll:

Row 1 (RS) Ko (8, 16, 4) sts before rep, work 40-st rep of Row 1 of Chart 1 (1, 1, 2) time(s), k23 (23, 23, 3) sts after rep, kfb – 1 st inc'd.

Row 2 Pfb, p24 (24, 24, 4) sts before rep, work 40-st rep of Row 2 of Chart 1 (1, 1, 2) time(s), po (8, 16, 4) sts after rep – 1 st inc'd.

Row 3 Ko (8, 16, 4) sts before rep, work 40-st rep of Row 3 of Chart 1 (1, 1, 2) time(s), k25 (25, 25, 5) sts after rep, kfb – 1 st inc'd.

Row 4 Pfb, p26 (26, 26, 6) sts before rep, work 40-st rep of Row 4 of Chart 1 (1, 1, 2) time(s), po (8, 16, 4) sts after rep.

Row 5 Ko (8, 16, 4) sts before rep, work 40-st rep of Row 5 of Chart 1 (1, 1, 2) time(s), k27 (27, 27, 7) sts after rep, kfb – 69 (77, 85, 93) sts.

Work 1 row straight.

Dec 1 st at beg of next row.

Work 5 rows straight.

Rep the last 6 rows 9 more times, then rep the dec row once more – 58 (66, 74, 82) sts rem.

Work straight until front measures 25 cm (9¾") from cast-on edge, ending with a WS row.

Shape armhole and front neck

Next row Cast off 7 (9, 11, 13) sts, work in established patt to last 2 sts, work 2 tog – 50 (56, 62, 68) sts rem.

Work 1 row straight.

Dec 1 st at armhole edge of the next 5 (7, 9, 11) rows, every RS row 8 (9, 9, 10) times, and AT THE SAME TIME dec 1 st at neck edge every 3 rows 13 (15, 17, 19) times – 24 (25, 27, 28) sts rem.

Work straight until front measures the same as back to shoulder shaping, ending at armhole edge.

Shape shoulder

Next row (RS) Cast off 2 (12, 13, 14) sts, work in patt to end – 12 (13, 14, 14) sts rem.

Work 1 row straight.

Cast off rem sts.

RIGHT FRONT

Using 3.25 mm (U.S. size 3) needles and A, cast on 64 (72, 80, 88) sts.

Purl 1 row.

Work in patt from Chart as foll:

Row 1 (RS) Kfb, k23 (23, 23, 3) sts before rep, work 40-st rep of Row 1 of Chart 1 (1, 1, 2) time(s), ko (8, 16, 4) sts after rep – 1 st inc'd.

Row 2 Po (8, 16, 4) sts before rep, work 40-st rep of Row 2 of Chart 1 (1, 1, 2) time(s), p24 (24, 24, 4) sts after rep, pfb – 1 st inc'd.

Row 3 Kfb, k25 (25, 25, 5) sts before rep, work 40-st rep of Row 3 of Chart 1 (1, 1, 2) time(s), ko (8, 16, 4) sts after rep – 1 st inc'd.

Row 4 Po (8, 16, 4) sts before rep, work 40-st rep of Row 4 of Chart 1 (1, 1, 2) time(s), p26 (26, 26, 6) sts after rep, pfb – 1 st inc'd.

Row 5 Kfb, k27 (27, 27, 7) sts before rep, work 40-st rep of Row 5 of Chart 1 (1, 1, 2) time(s), ko (8, 16, 4) sts after rep – 69 (77, 85, 93) sts.

Work 1 row straight.

Dec 1 st at end of next row.

Work 5 rows straight.

Rep the last 6 rows 9 more times, then rep the dec row once more – 58 (66, 74, 82) sts rem.

Work straight until front measures 25 cm (9¾") from cast-on edge, ending with a WS row.

Shape armhole and front neck

Next row Work 2 tog, work in established patt to end – 1 st dec'd.

Next row Cast off 7 (9, 11, 13) sts, work in established patt to end – 50 (56, 62, 68) sts rem.

Dec 1 st at armhole edge of the next 5 (7, 9, 11) rows, then every RS row 8 (9, 9, 10) times, and AT THE SAME TIME dec 1 st at neck edge every 3 rows 13 (15, 17, 19) times – 24 (25, 27, 28) sts rem.

Work straight until front measures the same as back to shoulder shaping, ending at armhole edge.

Shape shoulder

Next row (WS) Cast off 12 (12, 13, 14) sts, work in patt to end – 12 (13, 14, 14) sts rem.

Work 1 row straight.

Cast off rem sts.

SLEEVES

Using 3.25 mm (U.S. size 3) needles and A, cast on 96 (108, 120, 132) sts.

Purl 1 row.

Work in patt from Chart as foll:

Row 1 K8 (14, 0, 6) sts before rep, work 40-st rep of Row 1 of Chart 2 (2, 3, 3) times, k8 (14, 0, 6) sts after rep.

Row 2 P8 (14, 0, 6) sts before rep, work 40-st rep of Row 2 of Chart 2 (2, 3, 3) times, p8 (14, 0, 6) sts after rep.

Cont in established patt until sleeve measures 25 cm (9¾") from cast-on edge, ending with same patt row as back.

Shape top

Cast off 7 (9, 11, 13) sts at beg of next 2 rows – 82 (90, 98, 106) sts rem.

Work 2 rows straight.

Cast off 1 (2, 3, 4) st(s) at beg of next 2 rows – 80 (86, 92, 98) sts rem.

Dec 1 st at each end of the every RS row 10 times – 60 (66, 72, 78) sts rem.

Work 1 row straight.

Dec 1 st at each end of next row, then 4 rows twice – 54 (60, 66, 72) sts rem.

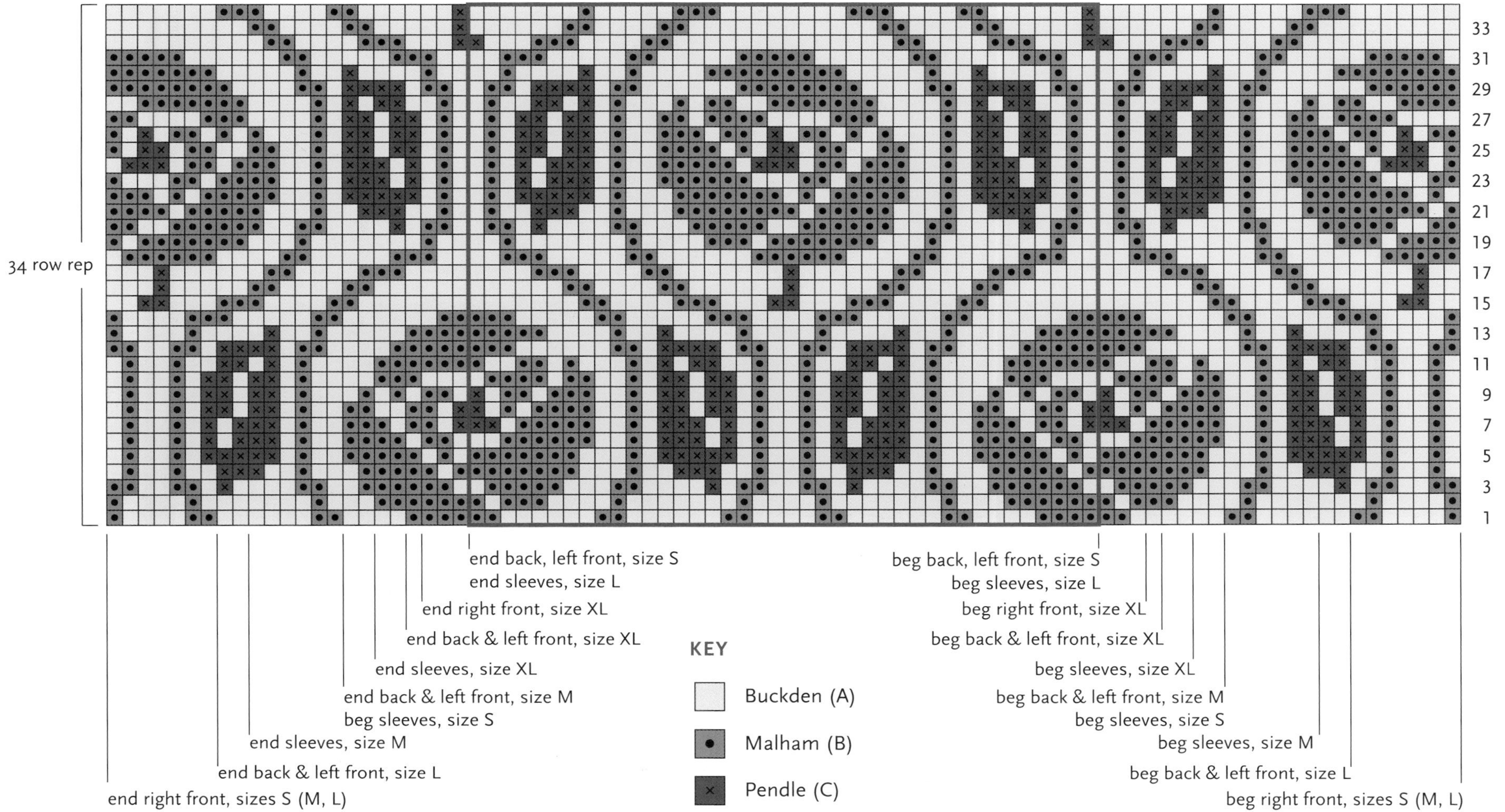

34 row rep

33
31
29
27
25
23
21
19
17
15
13
11
9
7
5
3
1

end back, left front, size S
end sleeves, size L
end right front, size XL
end back & left front, size XL
end sleeves, size XL
end back & left front, size M
beg sleeves, size S
end sleeves, size M
end back & left front, size L
end right front, sizes S (M, L)

beg back, left front, size S
beg sleeves, size L
beg right front, size XL
beg back & left front, size XL
beg sleeves, size XL
beg back & left front, size M
beg sleeves, size S
beg sleeves, size M
beg back & left front, size L
beg right front, sizes S (M, L)

KEY

- Buckden (A)
- Malham (B)
- Pendle (C)
- pattern repeat

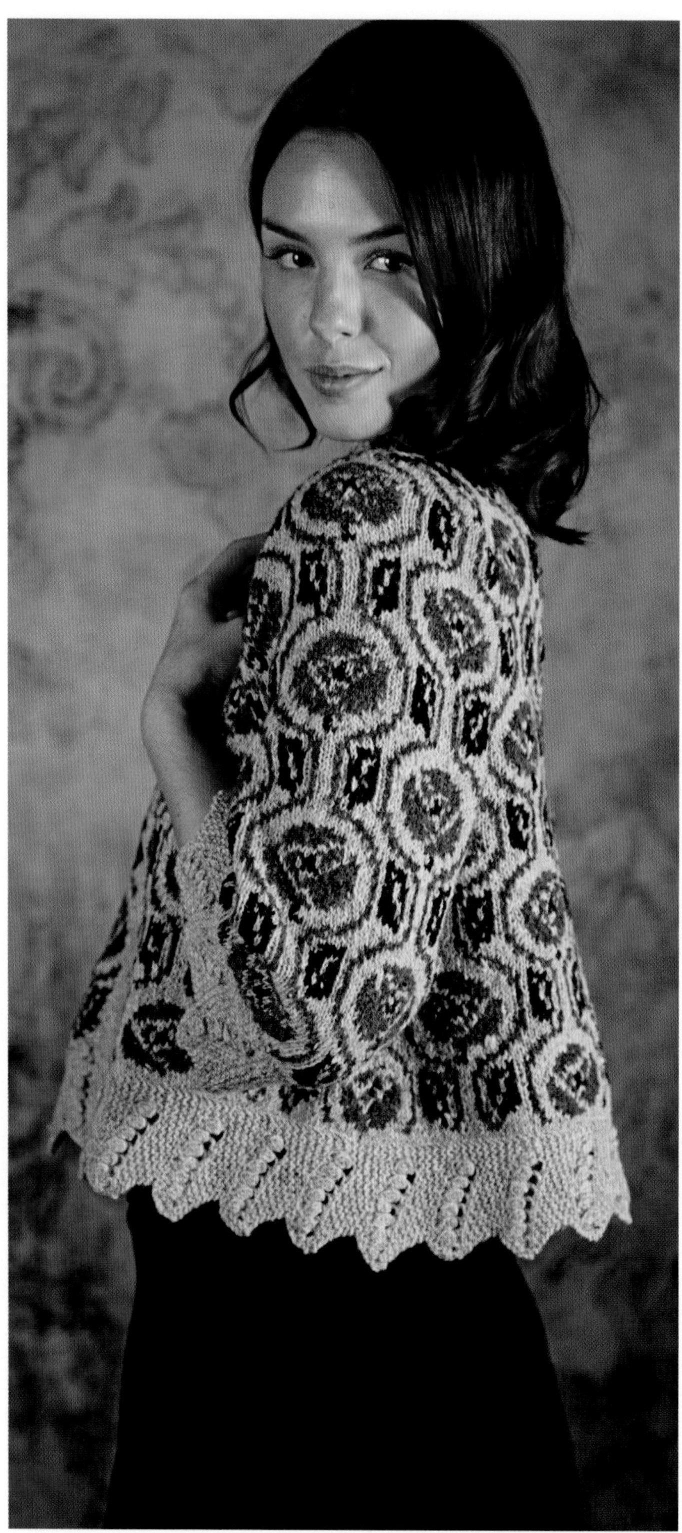

Dec 1 st at each end of next row, then every other row 3 times – 46 (52, 58, 64) sts rem.

Work 1 row straight.

Dec 1 st at each end of the next 6 (8, 10, 12) rows – 34 (36, 38, 40) sts rem.

Cast off 5 sts at beg of next 4 rows – 14 (16, 18, 20) sts rem.

Cast off rem sts.

EDGING

Using 3 mm needles and A, cast on 13 sts.

Row 1 K4, [yrn] twice, k2tog, k7 – 14 sts.

Row 2 K9, p1, k4.

Row 3 K3, MB, k2, [yrn] twice, k2tog, k6 – 15 sts.

Row 4 K8, p1, k6.

Row 5 K5, MB, k2, [yrn] twice, k2tog, k5 – 16 sts.

Row 6 K7, p1, k8.

Row 7 K7, MB, k2, [yrn] twice, k2tog, k4 – 17 sts.

Row 8 K6, p1, k10.

Row 9 K9, MB, k2, [yrn] twice, k2tog, k3 – 18 sts.

Row 10 K5, p1, k12.

Row 11 K11, MB, k2, [yrn] twice, k2tog, k2 – 19 sts.

Row 12 K4, p1, k14.

Row 13 K13, MB, k2, [yrn] twice, k2tog, k1 – 20 sts.

Row 14 K3, p1, k16.

Row 15 Knit.

Row 16 Cast off 7 sts, knit to end – 13 sts rem.

Rep Rows 1–16

until edging fits all round outside edges, easing around lower front corners, ending with Row 16.
Cast off rem sts.
Make 2 edgings to fit around lower edges of sleeves.

MAKING UP

Sew shoulder seams. Sew side and sleeve seams. Set in sleeves.
Sew straight edge of long edging to outside edges of body and neck, with cast-on and cast-off edges meeting at one side seam. Sew cast-on and cast-off edges together.
Sew straight edge of short edgings to lower edges of sleeves, with cast-on and cast-off edges meeting at underarm seam. Sew cast-on and cast-off edges together.

Caithness bag

An elegant but capacious knitted bag in 'Rowan Tweed', this is the perfect choice for carrying around your current favourite knitting project. The little spots around the lower part of the bag are knitted using the Fairisle technique, and have just two colours per row. The bag is lined in a toning plain cotton.

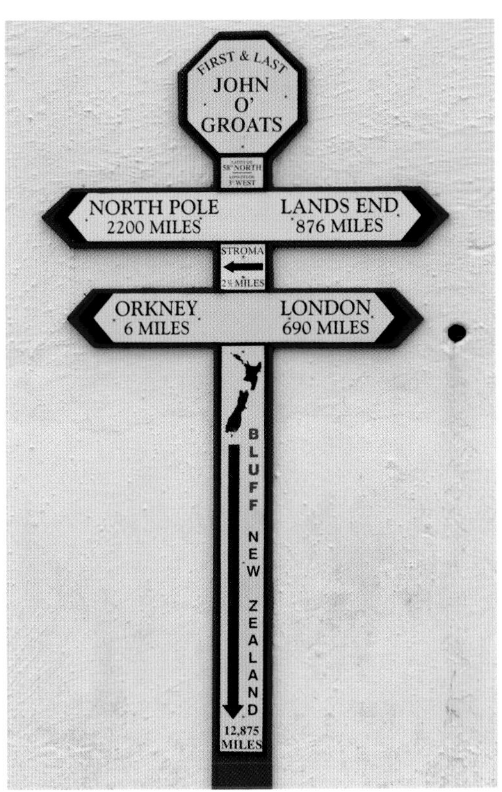

FINISHED SIZE
Approx 32 cm (12½") wide, 28 cm (11") high, and 14 cm (5½") deep at base

YARN
'Rowan Tweed' (100% wool; 118 m [129 yd]/50 g):
4 balls in Litton 592 (A)
1 ball each in Arncliffe 580 (B), Nidd 594 (C), Buckden 584 (D) and Settle 597 (E)

NEEDLES
Pair of 3.75 mm (U.S. size 5) knitting needles
Pair of 4 mm (U.S. size 6) knitting needles
Adjust needle size if necessary to obtain correct tension.

EXTRAS
125 cm (49") Petersham ribbon, 4 cm (1½") wide; 50 cm (19¾") long and 100 cm (39¼") wide lining fabric; plus optional lining fabric 34 x 32 cm (13½ x 12") for cardboard base; cardboard (optional) 14 x 32 cm (5½ x 12"); and sewing needle and matching thread

TENSION
21 sts and 28 rows = 10 cm (4") in St st using 4 mm (U.S. size 6) needles.

ABBREVIATIONS
See page 150.

NOTE
Slip stitches purlwise with yarn at the wrong side.

BAG

Base

Using 4 mm (U.S. size 6) needles and A, cast on 70 sts.

Beg with a RS row and work 21 rows in St st.

Gusset

Cast on 15 sts at beg of next 2 rows – 100 sts.

Next row (RS) P10, [M1, p9] 10 times – 110 sts.

Main part

Work Rows 1–42 of Patt chart. With A only, work 14 rows in St st, ending with a WS row.

Rib row 1 (RS) P2, [k2, p2] to end.

Rib Row 2 Knit.

Rep last 2 rows 20 more times.

Cast off in patt.

Work a second piece to match.

HANDLES (make 2)

Using 3.75 mm (U.S. size 5) needles and A, cast on 21 sts.

Row 1 (RS) K5, sl 1, k9, sl 1, k5.

Row 2 Purl.

Rep Rows 1 and 2 until piece measures 60 cm (23½"), ending with a WS row.

Cast off.

MAKING UP

Sew cast-on edges of both bag pieces together to form base.

Cut lining fabric to fit bag to bottom of rib section, using knitted piece as a template and adding seam allowances along all edges. Cut ribbon into two equal length pieces and pin along centre of WS of each handle. Sew edges of ribbon to handle along knitted slipped sts. Fold long edges of handle over ribbon, meeting in centre. Sew long edges together.

Sew bag side seams, reversing seam on rib section.

Sew base to side cast-on edges to form corner. Sew side and corner seams of lining same as for bag.

Place lining inside bag with WS together.

Fold top edge of lining to WS, and sew lining in place.

For extra stiffness in bottom of bag, cut a piece of cardboard to fit base. From lining make a 'bag' to fit cardboard. Sew long sides and one short end of bag tog. Insert cardboard and sew rem end tog. Place in base of bag.

Sew handles to each side of bag, with ends of handles at top of lining.

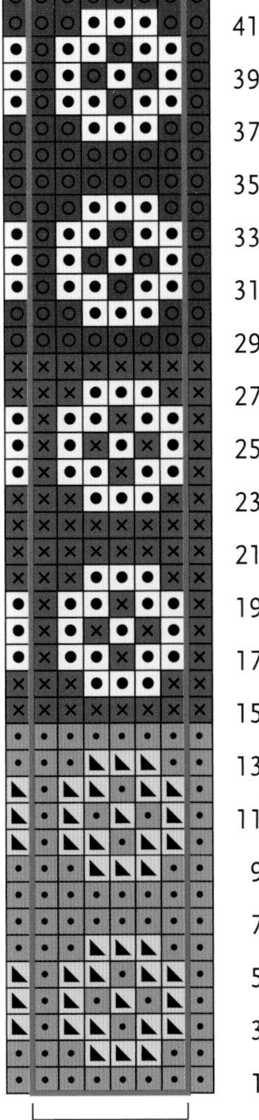

KEY

- Litton (A)
- Arncliffe (B)
- Nidd (C)
- Buckden (D)
- Settle (E)
- pattern repeat

Caithness socks

The neat rows of spots lend themselves to a really great pair of socks that are just the thing for country walks. They are knitted in 'Rowan Tweed', which is both soft and warm.

FINISHED SIZE
To fit shoe size U.K. 4–5 (6–7)
(U.S. 6½–7½ [8½–9½])
Foot circumference: 20.5 cm (8")

YARN
'Rowan Tweed' (100% wool; 118 m [129 yd]/50 g):
2 balls in Litton 592 (A)
1 ball each in Arncliffe 580 (B), Nidd 594 (C), Buckden 584 (D) and Settle 597 (E)

NEEDLES
3.25 mm (U.S. size 3) needles: straight and double-pointed needles (dpns)
Pair of 3.75 mm (U.S. size 5) knitting needles
Pair of 4 mm (U.S. size 6) knitting needles
Adjust needle size if necessary to obtain correct tension.

EXTRAS
Stitch markers; two safety pins.

TENSION

24 sts and 28 rows = 10 cm (4") in Patt Chart using 4 mm (U.S. size 6) needles;
24 sts and 32 rows = 10 cm (4") in stocking stitch using 3.75 mm (U.S. size 5) needles.

ABBREVIATIONS

See page 150.

SOCKS (make 2)

Using 3.25 mm (U.S. size 3) straight needles and A, cast on 62 sts.
Rib row 1 K2, [p2, k2] to end.
Rib row 2 P2, [k2, p2] to end.
Rep the last 2 rows twice more.
Change to 4 mm (U.S. size 6) needles.
Work Patt Chart Rows 1–40.
Change to 3.75 mm (U.S. size 5) needles.
Work Patt Chart Rows 41–70.
Cont in A only.
Next (dec) row K6, [k2tog, k2] to end – 48 sts rem.
Break yarn.
Divide sts onto 3 dpns with first 12 and last 12 sts on Needle 1, and 12 sts each on Needles 2 and 3.

Heel

With RS facing, join A to Needle 1.
Work on these 24 sts only, leaving rem 24 sts on hold for instep.
Beg with a RS row, work 13 rows of St st.

Shape heel

Row 1 (WS) Sl1, purl to end.
Row 2 Sl1, k13, ssk, k1, turn.
Row 3 Sl1, p5, p2tog, p1, turn.
Row 4 Sl1, k6, ssk, k1, turn.
Row 5 Sl1, p7, p2tog, p1, turn.
Row 6 Sl1, k8, ssk, k1, turn.
Row 7 Sl1, p9, p2tog, p1, turn.

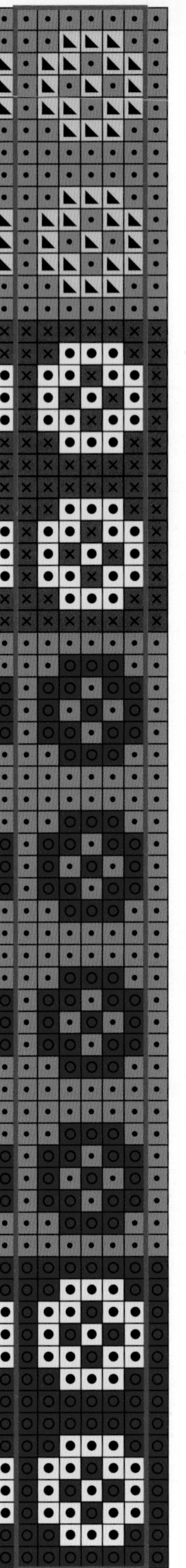

KEY

- Litton (A)
- Arncliffe (B)
- Nidd (C)
- Buckden (D)
- Settle (E)
- pattern repeat

Row 8 Sl1, k10, ssk, k1, turn.
Row 9 Sl1, p11, p2tog, p1, turn.
Row 10 Sl1, k12, ssk, turn.
Row 11 Sl1, p12, p2tog, turn – 14 sts rem.

Instep

With RS facing and A, k14 heel sts, pick up and k11 sts along side of heel, k1 from held instep sts, place marker (pm), k22 instep sts, pm, k1, pick up and k11 sts along other side of heel – 60 sts.

Arrange sts over 3 dpns with 18 sts each on Needles 1 and 3 (7 heel sts and 11 gusset sts), and 24 sts on Needle 2. Join to work in rnds. Pm for beg of rnd.

Rnd 1 Knit to 3 sts before m, k2tog, k1, sl m, knit to next m, sl m, k1, ssk, knit to end – 2 sts dec'd.

Rnd 2 Knit.

Rep the last 2 rnds 5 more times – 48 sts rem.

Slipping markers on every rnd, work straight until foot measures 18 (19) cm (7 [7½]") from back of heel.

Shape toe

Rnd 1 Knit to 4 sts before marker, k2tog, k2, sl m, ssk, knit to 2 sts before next m, k2tog, sl m, k2, ssk, knit to end – 4 sts dec'd.

Rnd 2 Knit.

Rep the last 2 rnds 5 more times – 24 sts rem.

Rearrange sts with first 6 sts on Needle 1, 12 sts on Needle 2, then rem 6 sts on Needle 1. Transfer the two groups of sts onto safety pins, fold sock inside out, then transfer the sts back onto two dpns. Cast off all sts using 3-needle cast off.

Ross cardigan

This classic Fairisle pattern is knitted in a lovely choice of colours in 'Rowan Fine Tweed': soft but quite distinct, bringing out the pattern to best advantage. The cardigan has a long, lean shape that gives it contemporary appeal.

FINISHED SIZE

	S	M	L	XL	
To fit bust					
	81.5–86.5	91.5–96.5	101.5–106.5	112–117	cm
	32–34	36–38	40–42	44–46	"

ACTUAL MEASUREMENTS

	S	M	L	XL	
Bust					
	91	103	115.5	130	cm
	35¾	40½	45½	51¼	"
Length to shoulder					
	64	66	68.5	70.5	cm
	25¼	26	27	27¾	"

Sleeve length 45 cm (17¾")

YARN

'Rowan Fine Tweed' (100% wool; 90 m [98 yd]/25 g):

5 (6, 6, 7) balls in Bedale 361 (A)

2 (2, 3, 3) balls each in Reeth 372 (B), Leyburn 383 (C), Nidd 382 (D), Bell Busk 376 (E) and Buckden 364 (G)

5 (5, 6, 6) balls in Bainbridge 369 (F)

1 (2, 2, 2) ball(s) in Hubberholme 370 (H)

NEEDLES

Pair of 3 mm (no exact U.S. equivalent; between U.S. size 2 and 3) knitting needles

Pair of 3.25 mm (U.S. size 3) knitting needles

Adjust needle size if necessary to obtain tension.

EXTRAS

Five buttons, 15 mm (⅝") Rowan BN1367.

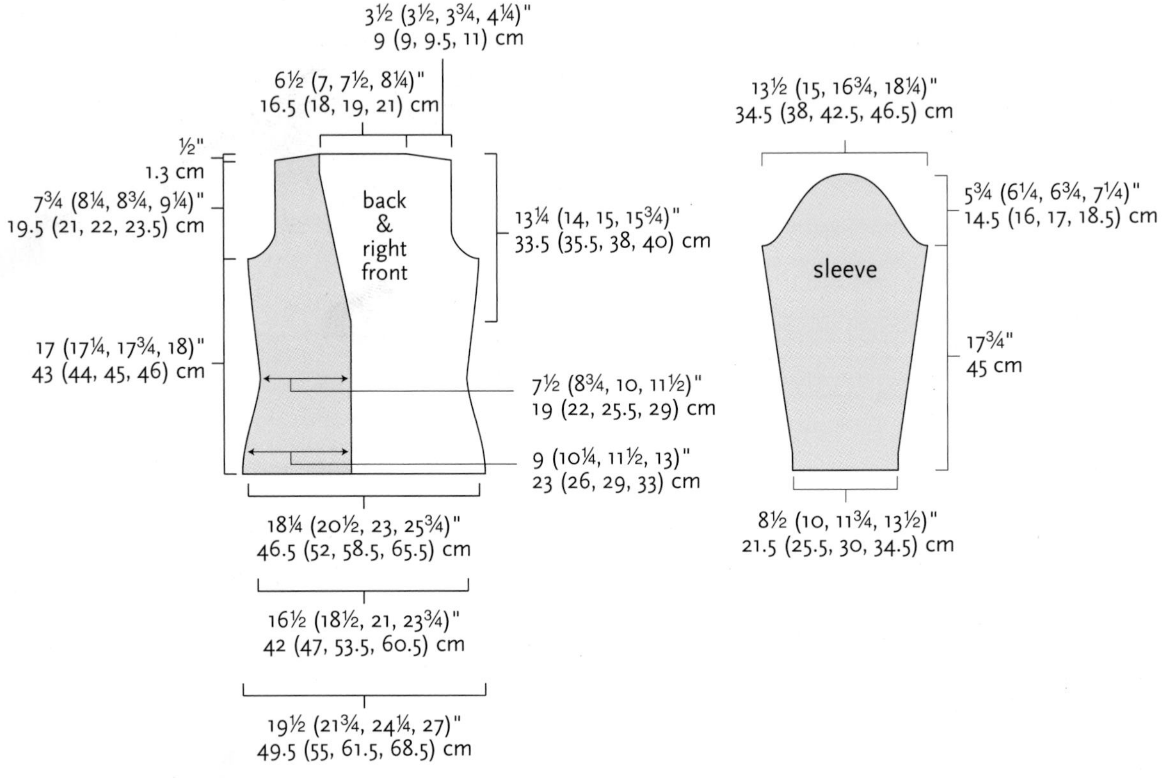

TENSION

29 sts and 33 rows = 10 cm (4") in colour patt using larger needles.

ABBREVIATIONS

See page 150.

NOTES

Read charts from right to left on RS rows and from left to right on WS rows. When working in patt, strand yarn not in use loosely across WS of work to keep fabric elastic.
When working from charts, use the Fairisle method (see page 149).

BACK

Using 3 mm needles and F, cast on 141 (157, 175, 195) sts.
Rib row 1 K1, [p1, k1] to end.
Rib row 2 P1, [k1, p1] to end.
Rep the last 2 rows 8 more times.
Change to 3.25 mm (U.S. size 3) needles.
Work in patt from Chart A as foll:
Row 1 (RS) Work 4 (6, 3, 1) st(s) before rep, work 12-st rep 11 (12, 14, 16) times, work 5 (7, 4, 2) sts after rep.
Row 2 Work 5 (7, 4, 2) sts before rep, work 12-st rep 11 (12, 14, 16) times, work 4 (6, 3, 1) st(s) after rep.
Work 2 more rows in established patt.
Dec 1 st at each end of the next row, then every 4 rows 10 more times – 119 (135, 153, 173) sts rem.
Work 17 rows straight.
Inc 1 st at each end of the next row, then every 8 rows 6 times – 133 (149, 167, 187) sts.
Work straight until back measures 43 (44, 45, 46) cm (17 [17¼, 17¾, 18]") from cast-on edge, ending with a WS row.

Shape armholes

Cast off 7 (9, 11, 13) sts at beg of next 2 rows – 119 (131, 145, 161) sts rem.
Dec 1 st at each end of the next 5 (7, 9, 11) rows, then every RS row 6 (7, 8, 9) times – 97 (103, 111, 121) sts rem.
Work straight until armhole measures 19.5 (21, 22, 23.5) cm (7¾ [8¼, 8¾, 9¼]"), ending with a WS row.

Shape shoulders

Cast off 12 (13, 14, 15) sts at beg of next 2 rows, then 13 (13, 14, 16) sts at beg of next 2 rows – 47 (51, 55, 59) sts rem.
Cast off rem sts.

LEFT FRONT

Using 3 mm and F, cast on 66 (74, 84, 94) sts.
Rib row 1 [K1, p1] to end.
Rep the last row 17 more times.
Change to 3.25 mm (U.S. size 3) needles.
Work in patt from Chart B as foll:
Row 1 (RS) Work 13 (21, 7, 17) sts before rep, work 24-st rep 2 (2, 3, 3) times, work 5 sts after rep.
Row 2 Work 5 sts before rep, work 24-st rep 2 (2, 3, 3) times, work 13 (21, 7, 17) sts after rep.
Work 2 more rows in established patt.
Dec 1 st at beg of the next row, then every 4 rows 10 more times – 55 (63, 73, 83) sts rem.
Work 17 rows straight.
Inc 1 st at beg of the next row, then every 8 rows 6 times, and AT THE SAME TIME when piece measures 30 cm (12") from cast-on edge, dec 1 st at neck edge on the next row, then every 4 rows 18 (20, 23, 25) times, and AT THE SAME TIME when front measures same as back to armhole shaping, end with a WS row.

CHART A: BACK, RIGHT FRONT, AND LEFT SLEEVE

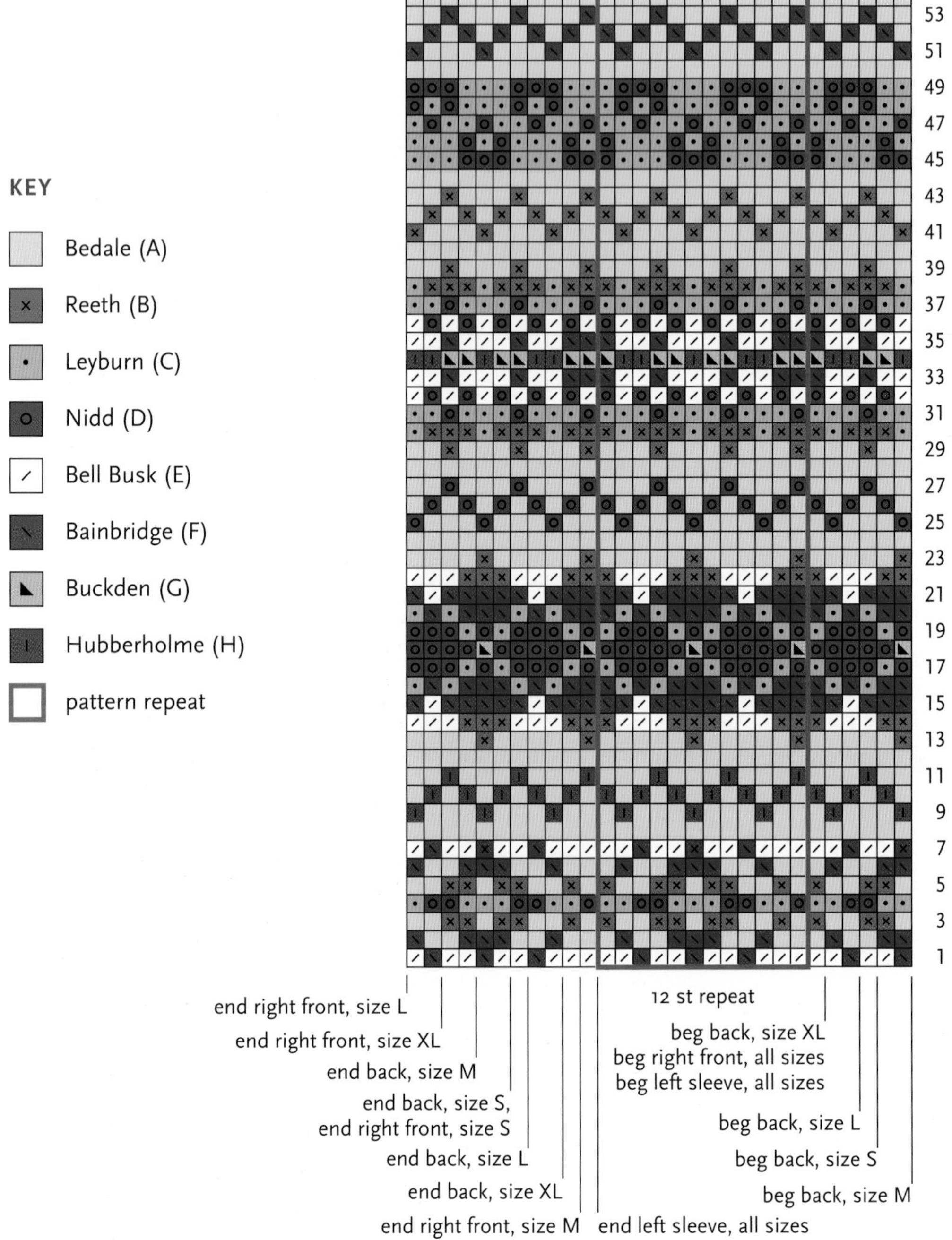

KEY
Bedale (A)
Reeth (B)
Leyburn (C)
Nidd (D)
Bell Busk (E)
Bainbridge (F)
Buckden (G)
Hubberholme (H)
pattern repeat
53
51
49
47
45
43
41
39
37
35
33
31
29
27
25
23
21
19
17
15
13
11
9
7
5
3
1
12 st repeat
end right front, size L
end right front, size XL
end back, size M
end back, size S, end right front, size S
end back, size L
end back, size XL
end right front, size M
end left sleeve, all sizes
beg back, size XL
beg right front, all sizes
beg left sleeve, all sizes
beg back, size L
beg back, size S
beg back, size M

CHART B: LEFT FRONT AND RIGHT SLEEVE

Shape armhole

Next row (RS) Cast off 7 (9, 11, 13) sts, work in patt to end.
Work 1 row straight.
Dec 1 st at armhole edge of the next 5 (7, 9, 11) rows, then every RS row 6 (7, 8, 9) times – 25 (26, 28, 31) sts rem when all shaping is complete.
Work straight until front measures the same as back to shoulder, ending with a WS row.

Shape shoulder

Next row (RS) Cast off 12 (13, 14, 15) sts, work in patt to end – 13 (13, 14, 16) sts rem.
Work 1 row straight.
Cast off rem sts.

RIGHT FRONT

Using 3 mm needles and F, cast on 66 (74, 84, 94) sts.
Rib row 1 [K1, p1] to end.
Rep the last row 17 more times.
Change to 3.25 mm (U.S. size 3) needles.
Work in patt from Chart A as foll:
Row 1 (RS) Work 1 st before rep, work 12-st rep 5 (6, 6, 7) times, work 5 (1, 11, 9) st(s) after rep.
Row 2 Work 5 (1, 11, 9) st(s) before rep, work 12-st rep 5 (6, 6, 7) times, work 1 st after rep.
Work 2 more rows in established patt.
Dec 1 st at end of the next row, then every 4 rows 10 more times – 55 (63, 73, 83) sts rem.
Work 17 rows straight.
Inc 1 st at end of the next row, then every 8 rows 6 times, AT THE SAME TIME when work measures 30 cm (12") from cast-on edge, dec 1 st at neck edge on the next row, then every 4 rows 18 (20, 23, 25) times, and AT THE SAME TIME when front measures same as back to armhole shaping, end with a RS row.

Shape armhole

Next row (WS) Cast off 7 (9, 11, 13) sts, work in patt to end.
Dec 1 st at armhole edge of the next 5 (7, 9, 11) rows, then every RS row 6 (7, 8, 9) times – 25 (26, 28, 31) sts rem when all shaping is complete.
Work straight until front measures the same as back to shoulder, ending with a RS row.

Shape shoulder

Next row (WS) Cast off 12 (13, 14, 15) sts, work in patt to end – 13 (13, 14, 16) sts rem.
Work 1 row straight.
Cast off rem sts.

LEFT SLEEVE

Using 3 mm needles and F, cast on 61 (73, 85, 97) sts.
Rib row 1 K1, [p1, k1] to end.
Rib row 2 P1, [k1, p1] to end.
Rep the last 2 rows 8 more times.
Change to 3.25 mm (U.S. size 3) needles.
Work in patt from Chart A as foll, starting with Row 29:
Row 1 (RS) Work 1 st before rep, work 12-st rep 5 (6, 7, 8) times.
Row 2 Work 12-st rep 5 (6, 7, 8) times, work 1 st after rep.
Cont patt as established and inc 1 st at each end of the next row, then every 8 rows 17 times – 97 (109, 121, 133) sts. Work new sts into patt.
Work straight until sleeve measures 45 cm (17¾") from cast-on edge, ending with same row as back to armhole shaping.

Shape cap

Cast off 7 (9, 13, 15) sts at beg of next 2 rows – 83 (89, 95, 103) sts rem.
Cast off 1 (2, 3, 4) st(s) at beg of next 2 rows

– 81 (87, 89, 95) sts rem.
Dec 1 st at each end of every RS row 10 times – 61 (67, 69, 75) sts rem.
Work 1 row straight.
Dec 1 st at each end of next row, then every 4 rows twice – 55 (61, 63, 69) sts rem.
Dec 1 st at each end of next row, then every other row 3 times – 47 (53, 55, 61) sts rem.
Work 1 row straight.
Dec 1 st at each end of the next 6 (8, 10, 12) rows – 35 (37, 35, 37) sts rem.
Cast off 5 sts at beg on next 4 rows – 15 (17, 15, 17) sts rem.
Cast off rem sts.

RIGHT SLEEVE

Using 3 mm needles and F, cast on 61 (73, 85, 97) sts.
Rib row 1 K1, [p1, k1] to end.
Rib row 2 P1, [k1, p1] to end.
Rep the last 2 rows 8 more times.
Change to 3.25 mm (U.S. size 3) needles.
Work in patt from Chart B as foll:
Row 1 (RS) Work 7 (1, 7, 1) st(s) before rep, work 24-st rep 2 (3, 3, 4) times, work 6 (0, 6, 0) sts after rep.
Row 2 Work 6 (0, 6, 0) sts before rep, work 24-st rep 2 (3, 3, 4) times, work 7 (1, 7, 1) st(s) after rep.
Cont in established patt and inc 1 st at each end of the next row, then every 8 rows 17 times – 97 (109, 121, 133) sts. Work new sts into patt.
Work straight until sleeve measures 45 cm (17¾"), ending with same row as left front to armhole shaping.

Shape cap

Cast off 7 (9, 13, 15) sts at beg of next 2 rows – 83 (89, 95, 103) sts rem.
Cast off 1 (2, 3, 4) st(s) at beg of next 2 rows – 81 (87, 89, 95) sts rem.
Dec 1 st at each end of every RS row 10 times – 61 (67, 69, 75) sts rem.
Work 1 row straight.
Dec 1 st at each end of next row, then every 4 rows twice – 55 (61, 63, 69) sts rem.
Dec 1 st at each end of next row, then every other row 3 times – 47 (53, 55, 61) sts rem.
Work 1 row straight.
Dec 1 st at each end of the next 6 (8, 10, 12) rows – 35 (37, 35, 37) sts rem.
Cast off 5 sts at beg on next 4 rows – 15 (17, 15, 17) sts rem.
Cast off rem sts.

BUTTON BAND

Sew shoulder seams.
Using 3.25 mm (U.S. size 3) needles and F, cast on 11 sts.
Row 1 (RS) K2, [p1, k1] 3 times, p1, k2.
Row 2 K1, [p1, k1] to end.
Rep the last 2 rows until band, when slightly stretched, fits along right front edge to centre of back neck, ending with a RS row.
Cast off all sts in rib.
Sew band in place.
Mark position for 5 buttons, the first 2 cm (¾") from cast-on edge, the 5th 2 cm (¾") below neck shaping, and evenly space the rem 3 in between.

BUTTONHOLE BAND

Using 3.25 mm (U.S. size 3) needles and F, cast on 11 sts.
Row 1 (RS) K2, [p1, k1] twice, p1, k2.
Row 2 K1, [p1, k1] to end.
Rep the last 2 rows twice more; piece should measure 2 cm (¾").

Buttonhole row Work 5 sts in established rib patt, k2tog, yrn, work to end.

Cont in rib, working rem buttonholes to match markers, then work straight until band, when slightly stretched, fits along left front edge to centre of back neck, ending with a RS row. Cast off all sts in rib.
Sew band in place. Sew ends of bands together where they meet at centre back neck.

MAKING UP

Sew side and sleeve seams. Set in sleeves. Sew on buttons.

Portree sweater

The really strong scroll pattern in bands of colour on this sweater has a special feature: it carries across the sleeves to give it even more impact. It is knitted in 'Rowan Tweed'. The polo neck, cuffs and hem are in simple rib.

FINISHED SIZE

S	M	L	XL	
To fit bust				
81.5–86.5	91.5–96.5	101.5–106.5	112–117	cm
32–34	36–38	40–42	44–46	"

ACTUAL MEASUREMENTS

Bust				
96	107.5	118.5	131	cm
37¾	42¼	46¾	51½	"
Length to shoulder				
59.5	61	61.5	63	cm
23½	24	24¼	24¾	"

Sleeve length 45 cm (17¾")

YARN

'Rowan Tweed' (100% wool; 118 m [129 yd]/50 g):
2 (2, 3, 3) balls in Arncliffe 580 (A)
3 (3, 4, 4) balls in Pendle 595 (B)
1 (2, 2, 2) ball(s) each in Reeth (C) and Hubberholme 589 (D)
2 (2, 2, 2) balls in Bainbridge 588 (E)

NEEDLES

Pair of 3.75 mm (U.S. size 5) knitting needles
Pair of 4 mm (U.S. size 6) knitting needles
Adjust needle size if necessary to obtain correct tension.

EXTRAS

Stitch holders.

TENSION

21 sts and 28 rows = 10 cm (4") in St st using larger needles.

ABBREVIATIONS

See page 150.

NOTES

Read charts from right to left on RS rows and from left to right on WS rows. Twist yarns on WS of row to avoid a hole.
When working from chart, use the Fairisle method (see page 149).

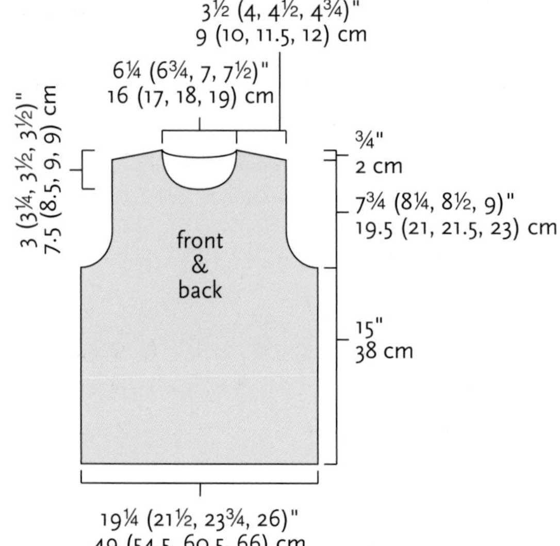

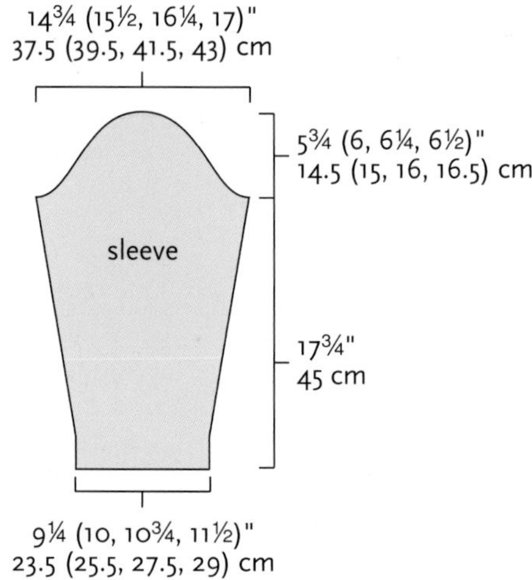

BACK

Using 3.75 mm (U.S. size 5) needles and B, cast on 101 (113, 125, 137) sts.

Rib row 1 K1, [p1, k1] to end.

Rib row 2 P1, [k1, p1] to end.

Rep the last 2 rows 6 more times.

Change to 4 mm (U.S. size 6) needles.

*Work in patt from Chart A as foll:

Row 1 Work 1 (7, 3, 9) st(s) before rep, work 20-st rep 5 (5, 6, 6) times, work 0 (6, 2, 8) sts after rep.

Row 2 Work 0 (6, 2, 8) sts before rep, work 20-st rep 5 (5, 6, 6) times, work 1 (7, 3, 9) st(s) after rep.

Cont in established patt to end of Row 23.

Work in patt from Chart B as foll:

Row 1 Work 2 sts before rep, work 12-st rep 8 (9, 10, 11) times, work 3 sts after rep.

Row 2 Work 3 sts before rep, work 12-st rep 8 (9, 10, 11) times, work 2 sts after rep.

Cont in established patt to end of Row 15.

Work in patt from Chart C as foll:

Row 1 Work 1 (7, 3, 9) st(s) before rep, work 20-st rep 5 (5, 6, 6) times, work 0 (6, 2, 8) sts after rep.

Row 2 Work 0 (6, 2, 8) sts before rep, work 20-st rep 5 (5, 6, 6) times, work 1 (7, 3, 9) st(s) after rep.

Cont in established patt to end of Row 48.

Rep from * until back measures 38 cm (15") from cast-on edge, ending with a WS row.

Shape armholes

Cast off 7 (8, 9, 10) sts at beg of next 2 rows – 87 (97, 107, 117) sts rem.

Dec 1 st at each end of next 3 (5, 7, 9) rows, then every RS row 5 times – 71 (77, 83, 89) sts rem.

Work straight until armhole measures 19.5 (21, 21.5, 23) cm (7¾ [8¼, 8½, 9]"), ending with a WS row.

Shape shoulders

Cast off 6 (7, 8, 9) sts at beg of next 2 rows – 59 (63, 67, 71) sts rem.

Shape back neck

Next row Cast off 6 (7, 8, 9) sts, work in established patt until there are 10 sts on right needle, turn, leaving rem 43 (46, 49, 52) sts on hold.

Next row Cast off 3 sts, work in patt to end.

Cast off rem 7 sts.

With RS facing, sl next 27 (29, 31, 33) sts to holder, rejoin yarn to rem 16 (17, 18, 19) sts, work in established patt to end.

Next row Cast off 6 (7, 8, 9) sts, work in patt to end – 10 sts rem.

Next row Cast off 3 sts, work in patt to end.

Cast off rem 7 sts.

FRONT

Work as given for Back until armhole measures 12 (12.5, 12.5, 14) cm (4¾ [5, 5, 5½]"), ending with a WS row.

Shape front neck

Next row Work 25 (27, 29, 31) sts in established patt, turn, leaving rem 46 (50, 54, 58) sts on hold.

Dec 1 st at neck edge every row 4 times, then every RS row 2 times – 19 (21, 23, 25) sts rem.

Work straight until Front measures the same as Back to shoulder shaping, ending at armhole edge.

Shape left shoulder

Cast off 6 (7, 8, 9) sts at beg of next 2 RS rows – 7 sts rem.

Work 1 row straight.

Cast off rem sts.

With RS facing, sl next 21 (23, 25, 27) sts to holder, rejoin yarn to rem 25 (27, 29, 31) sts,

CHART A

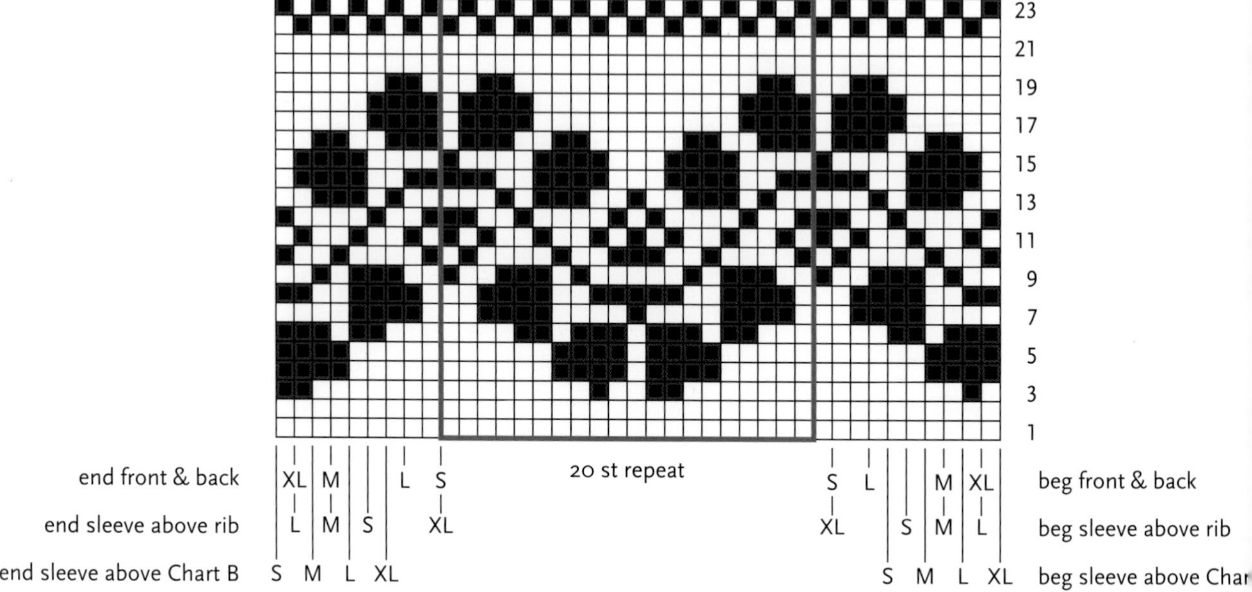

23
21
19
17
15
13
11
9
7
5
3
1
end front & back
XL M L S
20 st repeat
S L M XL
beg front & back
end sleeve above rib
L M S XL
XL S M L
beg sleeve above rib
end sleeve above Chart B
S M L XL
S M L XL
beg sleeve above Char

CHART B

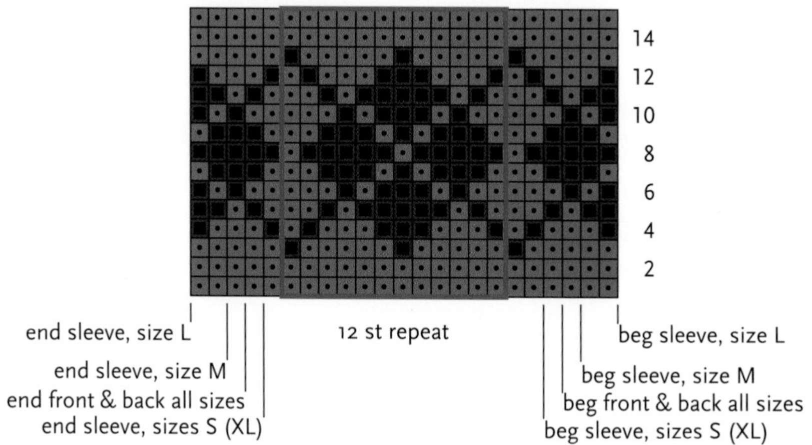

14
12
10
8
6
4
2
end sleeve, size L
end sleeve, size M
end front & back all sizes
end sleeve, sizes S (XL)
12 st repeat
beg sleeve, size L
beg sleeve, size M
beg front & back all sizes
beg sleeve, sizes S (XL)

CHART C

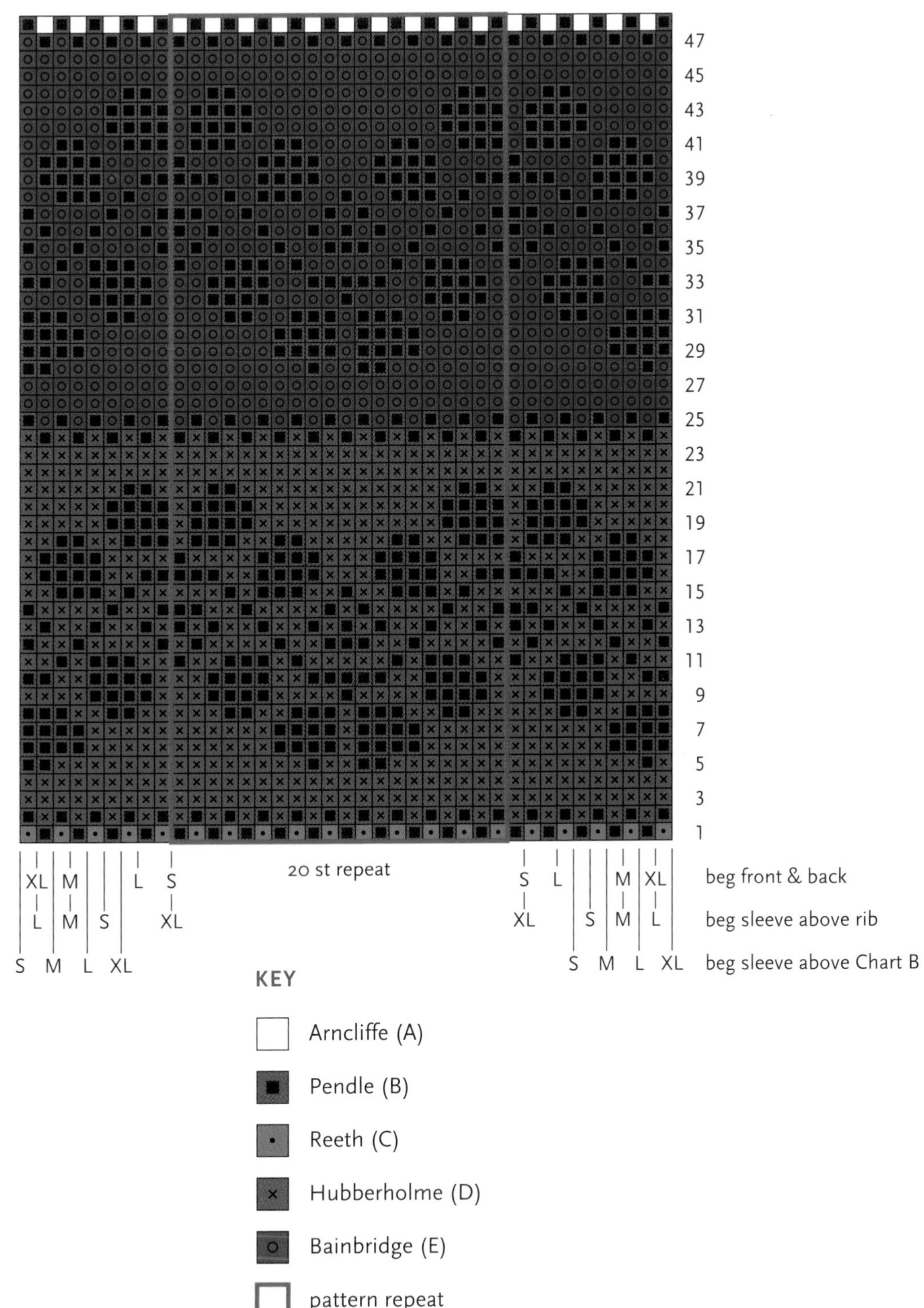

47
45
43
41
39
37
35
33
31
29
27
25
23
21
19
17
15
13
11
9
7
5
3
1
20 st repeat
end front & back
XL M L S
end sleeve above rib
L M S XL
end sleeve above Chart B
S M L XL
beg front & back
S L M XL
beg sleeve above rib
XL S M L
beg sleeve above Chart B
S M L XL
KEY
Arncliffe (A)
Pendle (B)
Reeth (C)
Hubberholme (D)
Bainbridge (E)
pattern repeat

work in established patt to end.
Dec 1 st at neck edge every row 4 times, then every RS row 2 times – 19 (21, 23, 25) sts rem.
Work straight until Front measures the same as Back to shoulder shaping, ending at armhole edge.

Shape right shoulder

Cast off 6 (7, 8, 9) sts at beg of next 2 WS rows – 7 sts rem.
Work 1 row straight.
Cast off rem sts.

SLEEVES

Using 3.75 mm (U.S. size 5) needles and B, cast on 49 (53, 57, 61) sts.
Rib row 1 K1, [p1, k1] to end.
Rib row 2 P1, [k1, p1] to end.
Rep the last 2 rows 6 more times.
Change to 4 mm (U.S. size 6) needles.
Beg at Row 26 and work from Chart C as foll:
Row 1 Work 5 (7, 9, 1) st(s) before rep, work 20-st rep of Row 26 two (two, two, three) times, work 4 (6, 8, 0) sts after rep.
Row 2 Work 4 (6, 8, 0) sts before rep, work 20-st rep of Row 27 five (five, six, six) times, work 5 (7, 9, 1) st(s) after rep.
Work straight for 6 more rows.
Inc 1 st at each end of the next row, then every 6 rows 2 times – 55 (59, 63, 67) sts.
Work straight for 2 more rows, ending with Row 48 of Chart C.
Work in patt from Chart A as foll:
Next row (WS) Work 7 (9, 1, 3) st(s) before rep, work 20-st rep of Row 1 two (two, two, three) times, work 8 (10, 2, 4) sts after rep.
Next row Work 8 (10, 2, 4) sts before rep, work 20-st rep of Row 2 two (two, two, three) times, work 7 (9, 1, 3) st(s) after rep.
Work straight for 1 more row.
Inc 1 st at each end of the next row, then every 8 rows 3 more times – 63 (67, 71, 75) sts.
Work 1 row straight, ending with Row 23 of Chart A.
Work in patt from Chart B as foll:
Next row (RS) Work 2 (4, 6, 2) sts before rep, work 12-st rep of Row 1 five (five, five, six) times, work 1 (3, 5, 1) st(s) after rep.
Next row Work 1 (3, 5, 1) st(s) before rep, work 12-st rep of Row 2 five (five, five, six) times, work 2 (4, 6, 2) sts after rep.
Work 4 rows straight.
Inc 1 st at each end of the next row, then every 8 rows once more, ending with Row 15 of Chart B – 67 (71, 75, 79) sts.
Work in patt from Chart C as foll:
Next row (WS) Work 3 (5, 7, 9) sts before rep, work 20-st rep of Row 1 five times, work 4 (6, 8, 10) sts after rep.
Next row Work 4 (6, 8, 10) sts before rep, work 20-st rep of Row 2 five times, work 3 (5, 7, 9) sts after rep.
Work 5 rows straight.
Inc 1 st at each end of the next row, then and every 8 rows 4 more times – 77 (81, 85, 89) sts.
Work straight until sleeve measures 45 cm (17¾") from cast-on edge, ending with same row as back and front to armhole shaping.

Shape sleeve top

Cast off 7 (8, 9, 10) sts at beg of next 2 rows – 63 (65, 67, 69) sts rem.
Dec 1 st at each end of next 3 rows, every RS row 3 times, every 4 rows 4 times, every RS row 4 (5, 6, 7) times, then every row 5 times – 25 sts rem.
Cast off rem sts.

COLLAR

Sew right shoulder seam.
With RS facing, using 3.75 mm (U.S. size 5)

needles and B, pick up and k21 sts along left front neck edge, k21 (23, 25, 27) held front neck sts, pick up and k21 sts along right front neck edge, 6 sts along right back neck edge, k27 (29, 31, 33) held back neck sts, then pick up and k6 sts along left back neck edge – 102 (106, 110, 114) sts.

Rib row [K1, p1] to end.

Rep the last row until collar measures 7.5 cm (3").

Change to 4 mm (U.S. size 6) needles.

Cont in established rib until collar measures 21 cm (8¼").

Cast off loosely in rib.

MAKING UP

Sew left shoulder and collar seam, reversing seam on Collar. Sew side and sleeve seams. Sew in sleeves.

Peebles stole

This beautiful stole is knitted in 'Rowan Fine Tweed', a 100 per cent wool yarn with a light fleck in it, shown here in a rich green. It has four different stitch panels, featuring a mixture of cable and lace stitches, and it is finished with a pretty fluted edging. It makes a wonderfully warm but light wrap for cooler days or evenings. The fluted edging stands up slightly to make a face-framing collar.

FINISHED SIZE
40.5 cm (16") wide and 160 cm (63") long, excluding edging

YARN
17 balls of 'Rowan Fine Tweed' (100% wool; 90 m [98 yd]/25 g) in Richmond 381

NEEDLES
Pair of 3.25 mm (U.S. size 3) knitting needles
Adjust needle size if necessary to obtain correct tension.

EXTRAS
Cable needle (cn)

TENSION

28 sts and 36 rows = 10 cm (4") in St st.

ABBREVIATIONS

C4B: slip 2 sts to cn and hold in back of work, k2, k2 from cn.
C4F: slip 2 sts to cn and hold in front of work, k2, k2 from cn.
Wyib: with yarn in back.
Wyif: with yarn in front.
See also page 150.

PATT PANEL A (panel of 8 sts)

Row 1 (RS) K1, yf, k2tog, k5.
Row 2 and all WS rows Purl.
Row 3 K2, yf, k2tog, k4.
Row 5 K3, yf, k2tog, k3.
Row 7 K4, yf, k2tog, k2.
Row 9 K5, yf, k2tog, k1.
Row 11 K6, yf, k2tog.
Row 13 K5, skp, yf, k1.
Row 15 K4, skp, yf, k2.
Row 17 K3, skp, yf, k3.
Row 19 K2, skp, yf, k4.
Row 21 K1, skp, yf, k5.
Row 23 Skp, yf, k6.
Row 24 Purl.
Rep Rows 1–24 for patt.

PATT PANEL B (panel of 4 sts)

Row 1 (RS) K2, yf, k2tog.
Row 2 P2, yf, k2tog.
Rows 3–6 Rep Rows 1 and 2 twice more.
Row 7 C4F.
Row 8 Rep Row 2.
Rows 9–12 Rep Rows 1 and 2 twice more.
Rep Rows 1–12 for patt.

PATT PANEL C (multiple of 10 sts + 1)

Row 1 (RS) K1, *yf, k3, sk2p, k3, yf, k1; rep from *.
Row 2 Purl.
Row 3 P1, *k1, yf, k2, sk2p, k2, yf, k1, p1; rep from *.
Rows 4 and 6 K1, *p9, k1; rep from *.
Row 5 P1, *k2, yf, k1, sk2p, k1, yf, k2, p1; rep from *.
Row 7 P1, *k3, yf, sk2p, yf, k3, p1; rep from *.
Row 8 Purl.
Rep Rows 1–8 for patt.

PATT PANEL D (panel of 8 sts)

Row 1 (RS) K5, skp, yf, k1.
Row 2 and all WS rows Purl.
Row 3 K4, skp, yf, k2.
Row 5 K3, skp, yf, k3.
Row 7 K2, skp, yf, k4.
Row 9 K1, skp, yf, k5.
Row 11 Skp, yf, k6.
Row 13 K1, yf, k2tog, k5.
Row 15 K2, yf, k2tog, k4.
Row 17 K3, yf, k2tog, k3.
Row 19 K4, yf, k2tog, k2.
Row 21 K5, yf, k2tog, k1.
Row 23 K6, yf, k2tog.
Row 24 Purl.
Rep Rows 1–24 rows for patt.

STOLE

Cast on 119 sts.
Row 1 (RS) P2, k4, p1, k4, p2, work Row 1 of Panel A over next 8 sts, p2, work Row 1 of Panel B over next 4 sts, p2, work Row 1 of Panel C over next 61 sts, p2, work Row 1 of Panel B over next 4 sts, p2, work Row 1 of Panel D over next 8 sts, p2, k4, p1, k4, p2.
Row 2 K2, p4, k1, p4, k2, work Row 2 of Panel D over next 8 sts, k2, work Row 2 of Panel B over next 4 sts, k2, work Row 2 of Panel C over next 61 sts, k2, work Row 2 of Panel B over next 4 sts, k2, work Row 2 of Panel A over next 8 sts, k2, p4, k1, p4, k2.

Rows 3 and 4 Work in established patt.
Row 5 P2, C4F, p1, C4F, p2, work in patt to last 13 sts, p2, C4B, p1, C4B, p2.
Row 6 K2, p4, k1, p4, k2, work in patt to last 13 sts, k2, p4, k1, p4, k2.
Cont in established patt, cross side cables every 6 rows and work until piece measures 160 cm (63") from cast on, ending with Row 8 of Panel C.
Cast off.

EDGING

Cast on 13 sts.
Row 1 Knit.
Row 2 P10, sl 1 wyib, turn.
Row 3 Sl 1 wyib, k10.
Row 4 P10, k3.
Row 5 K3, p10.
Row 6 K10, sl 1 wyif, turn.
Row 7 Sl 1 wyif, p10.
Row 8 Knit.
Rep Rows 1–8 for patt.
Cont in patt until shorter edge fits around 4 sides of stole.
Cast off.

MAKING UP

Weave in ends. Block stole to finished measurements.
Join cast-on and cast-off edges of edging.
Sew shorter edge to outside edges of stole.

Highland tunic

Another great project for cable enthusiasts. Its three-quarter length is just right for wearing over trousers or leggings, or a short pencil skirt. Knitted in 'Rowan Tweed', a double knitting yarn, it knits up relatively quickly.

FINISHED SIZE

	S	M	L	XL	
To fit bust					
	81.5–86.5	91.5–96.5	101.5–106.5	112–117	cm
	32–34	36–38	40–42	44–46	"
ACTUAL MEASUREMENTS					
Bust					
	95.5	106	117.5	128.5	cm
	37½	41¾	46¼	50½	"
Length to shoulder					
	73	75.5	77.5	80	cm
	28¾	29¾	30½	31½	"

YARN

11 (12, 13, 14) balls of 'Rowan Tweed' (100% wool; 118 m [129 yd]/50 g) in Hawes 582

NEEDLES

Pair of 3.25 mm (U.S. size 3) knitting needles
Pair of 4 mm (U.S. size 6) knitting needles
Adjust needle size if necessary to obtain correct tension.

EXTRAS
Cable needle (cn); locking markers (m); stitch holders.

TENSION
22 sts and 30 rows = 10 cm (4") in stocking stitch using larger needles.

ABBREVIATIONS
C6B: slip next 3 sts onto cn and hold in back of work, k3 then k3 from cn.
C6F: slip next 3 sts onto cn and hold in front of work, k3 then k3 from cn.
C4R: slip next st onto cn and hold in back of work, k3, then k1 from cn.
C4L: slip next 3 sts onto cn and hold in front of work, k1, then k3 from cn.
T4R: slip next 2 sts onto cn and hold in back of work, k2, then p2 from cn.
T4L: slip next 2 sts onto cn and hold in front of work, p2, then k2 from cn.
See also page 150.

PATT PANEL A (20 sts)
Row 1 (RS) P8, [k2, p2] 3 times.
Row 2 [K2, p2] 3 times, k8.
Row 3 P6, [T4R] 3 times, p2.
Row 4 K4, [p2, k2] twice, p2, k6.
Row 5 P4, [T4R] 3 times, p4.
Row 6 K6, [p2, k2] twice, p2, k4.
Row 7 P2, [T4R] 3 times, p6.
Row 8 K8, [p2, k2] 3 times.
Row 9 [P2, k2] 3 times, p8.
Row 10 Rep Row 8.
Row 11 P2, [T4L] 3 times, p6.
Row 12 Rep Row 6.
Row 13 P4, [T4L] 3 times, p4.
Row 14 Rep Row 4.
Row 15 P6, [T4L] 3 times, p2.
Row 16 Rep Row 2.
Rep Rows 1–16 for patt.

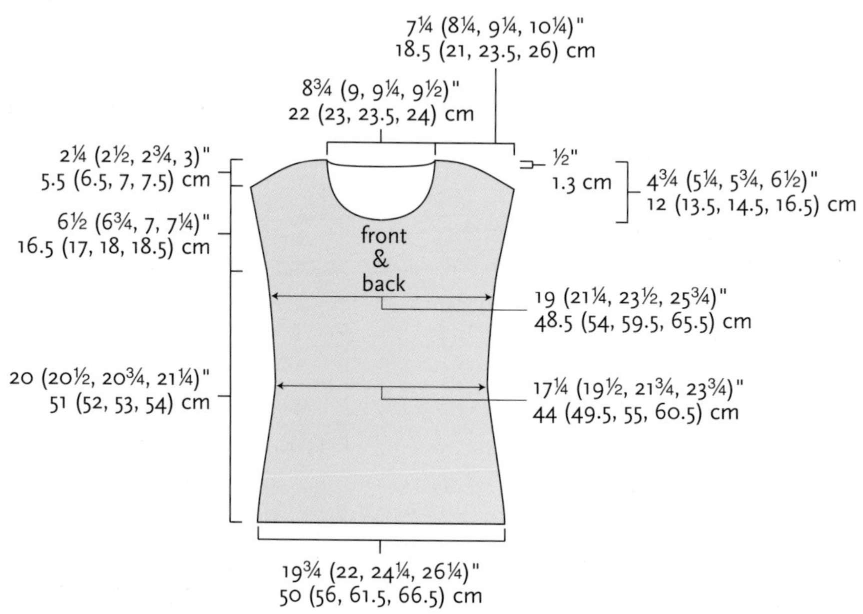

PATT PANEL B (12 sts)
Row 1 (RS) K1, p2, k6, p2, k1.
Row 2 P1, k2, p6, k2, p1.
Row 3 K1, p2, C6F, p2, k1.
Row 4 Rep Row 2.
Row 5 Rep Row 1.
Row 6 Rep Row 2.
Rep Rows 1–6 for patt.

PATT PANEL C (42 sts)
Row 1 (RS) [P2, k3] 3 times, p3, C6F, p3, [k3, p2] 3 times.
Row 2 [K2, p3] 3 times, k3, p6, k3, [p3, k2] 3 times.
Row 3 [P2, k3] 3 times, p2, C4R, C4L, p2, [k3, p2] 3 times.
Row 4 [K2, p3] 8 times, k2.
Row 5 [P2, k3] 8 times, p2.
Row 6 [K2, p3] 8 times, k2.
Row 7 [P2, k3] 3 times, p2, C4L, C4R, p2, [k3, p2] 3 times.
Row 8 [K2, p3] 3 times, k3, p6, k3, [p3, k2] 3 times.
Row 9 [P2, k3] twice, p2, C4L, p2, C6F, p2, C4R, p2, [k3, p2] twice.
Row 10 [K2, p3] twice, k3, p3, k2, p6, k2, p3, k3, [p3, k2] twice.
Row 11 P2, k3, [p2, C4L] twice, C4R, C4L, [C4R, p2] twice, k3, p2.
Row 12 K2, [p3, k3] twice, p6, k2, p6, [k3, p3] twice, k2.
Row 13 P2, [C4L, p2] twice, [C6B, p2] twice [C4R, p2] twice.
Row 14 [K3, p3] twice, [k2, p6] twice, k2, [p3, k3] twice.
Row 15 P3, C4L, p2, [C4L, C4R] 3 times, p2, C4R, p3.
Row 16 K4, p3, k3, [p6, k2] twice, p6, k3, p3, k4.
Row 17 P4, C4L, [p2, C6F] 3 times, p2, C4R, p4.
Row 18 K5, p3, k2, [p6, k2] 3 times, p3, k5.
Row 19 P5, [C4L, C4R] 4 times, p5.
Row 20 K6, [p6, k2] 3 times, p6, k6.
Row 21 P6, [C6B, p2] 3 times, C6B, p6.
Row 22 Rep Row 20.
Row 23 P5, [C4R, C4L] 4 times, p5.
Row 24 Rep Row 18.
Row 25 P5, k3, p2, [C6F, p2] 3 times, k3, p5.
Row 26 Rep Row 18.
Row 27 P5, [C4L, C4R] 4 times, p5.
Row 28 Rep Row 20.
Row 29 Rep Row 21.
Row 30 Rep Row 20.
Row 31 Rep Row 23.
Row 32 Rep Row 18.
Row 33 P4, C4R, [p2, C6F] 3 times, p2, C4L, p4.
Row 34 Rep Row 16.
Row 35 P3, C4R, p2, [C4R, C4L] 3 times, p2, C4L, p3.
Row 36 Rep Row 14.
Row 37 P2, [C4R, p2] twice, [C6B, p2] twice, [C4L, p2] twice.
Row 38 Rep Row 12.
Row 39 P2, k3, [p2, C4R] twice, C4L, C4R, [C4L, p2] twice, k3, p2.
Row 40 Rep Row 10.
Row 41 [P2, k3] twice, p2, C4R, p2, C6F, p2, C4L, p2, [k3, p2] twice.
Row 42 Rep Row 8.
Rows 43–48 Rep Rows 3–8.
Rep Rows 1–48 for patt.

PATT PANEL D (20 sts)
Row 1 (RS) [P2, k2] 3 times, p8.
Row 2 K8, [p2, k2] 3 times.
Row 3 P2, [T4L] 3 times, p6.
Row 4 K6, [p2, k2] twice, p2, k4.
Row 5 P4, [T4L] 3 times, p4.
Row 6 K4, [p2, k2] twice, p2, k6.
Row 7 P6, [T4L] 3 times, p2.

Row 8 [K2, p2] 3 times, k8.
Row 9 P8, [k2, p2] 3 times.
Row 10 Rep Row 8.
Row 11 P6, [T4R] 3 times, p2.
Row 12 Rep Row 6.
Row 13 P4, [T4R] 3 times, p4.
Row 14 Rep Row 4.
Row 15 P2, [T4R] 3 times, p6.
Row 16 Rep Row 2.
Rep Rows 1–16 for patt.

BACK

Using 3.25 mm (U.S. size 3) needles, cast on 138 (150, 162, 174) sts.
Rib row 1 P0 (2, 0, 2), [k2, p2] 9 (10, 12, 13) times, k1, p2, [k2, p2] twice, k1, [p2, k3] 8 times, p2, k1, p2, [k2, p2] twice, k1, [p2, k2] 9 (10, 12, 13) times, p0 (2, 0, 2).
Rib row 2 K0 (2, 0, 2), [p2, k2] 9 (10, 12, 13) times, p1, k2, [p2, k2] twice, p1, [k2, p3] 8 times, k2, p1, k2, [p2, k2] twice, p1, [k2, p2] 9 (10, 12, 13) times, k0 (2, 0, 2).
Work 14 more rows in established rib patt.
Change to 4 mm (U.S. size 6) needles.
Row 1 K16 (22, 28, 34), work across Row 1 of Panels A, B, C, B, then D, k16 (22, 28, 34).
Row 2 P16 (22, 28, 34), work across Row 2 of Panels D, B, C, B, then A, p16 (22, 28, 34).
Keeping sts before and after cable panels in St st, work 2 more rows in established patt.
Next (dec) row K4, skp, work in patt to last 6 sts, k2tog, k4 – 2 sts dec'd.
Work 9 rows straight.
Rep the last 10 rows 5 more times, then rep dec row once more – 124 (136, 148, 160) sts rem.
Work 17 rows straight.
Next (inc) row K4, M1, work in patt to last 4 sts, M1, k4 – 2 sts inc'd.
Work 9 rows straight.
Rep the last 10 rows 3 more times, then rep inc row once more – 134 (146, 158, 170) sts.
Work straight until back measures 51 (52, 53, 54) cm (20 [20½, 20¾, 21¼]") from cast on, ending with a WS row.
Mark each end of last row with locking m.

Shape cap sleeves

Row 1 K12 (18, 24, 30), M1, work in patt to last 12 (18, 24, 30) sts, M1, k12 (18, 24, 30) – 2 sts inc'd.
Work 3 rows straight, working inc sts in St st.
Row 5 K13 (19, 25, 31), M1, work in patt to last 13 (19, 25, 31) sts, M1, k13 (19, 25, 31) – 2 sts inc'd.
Work 3 rows straight.
Row 9 K14 (20, 26, 32), M1, work in patt to last 14 (20, 26, 32) sts, M1, k14 (20, 26, 32) – 2 sts inc'd.
Rep inc row every 4 rows 9 more times – 158 (170, 182, 194) sts.
Work 3 (5, 7, 9) rows straight.

Shape upper sleeve

Cast off 4 sts at beg of next 14 (16, 18, 20) rows – 102 (106, 110, 114) sts rem.

Shape shoulders and back neck

Next row Cast off 9 sts, work in patt until there are 12 (13, 14, 15) sts on right needle, turn, leaving rem 81 (84, 87, 90) sts on hold.
Next row Cast off 3 sts, work in patt to end – 9 (10, 11, 12) sts rem.
Cast off rem sts.
With RS facing, rejoin yarn to rem sts, cast off next 60 (62, 64, 66) sts, work in patt to end – 21 (22, 23, 24) sts rem.
Next row Cast off 9 sts, work in patt to end – 12 (13, 14, 15) sts rem.
Next row Cast off 3 sts, work in patt to end – 9 (10, 11, 12) sts rem.
Cast off rem sts.

POCKET LININGS (make 2)
Using 3.25 mm (U.S. size 3) needles, cast on 34 sts.
Beg with a knit row, work 46 rows in St st; piece should measure 16 cm (6¼").
Place sts on a holder.

FRONT
Using 3.25 mm (U.S. size 3) needles, cast on 138 (150, 162, 174) sts.
Rib row 1 P0 (2, 0, 2), [k2, p2] 9 (10, 12, 13) times, k1, p2, [k2, p2] twice, k1, [p2, k3] 8 times, p2, k1, p2, [k2, p2] twice, k1, [p2, k2] 9 (10, 12, 13) times, p0 (2, 0, 2).
Rib row 2 K0 (2, 0, 2), [p2, k2] 9 (10, 12, 13) times, p1, k2, [p2, k2] twice, p1, [k2, p3] 8 times, k2, p1, k2, [p2, k2] twice, p1, [k2, p2] 9 (10, 12, 13) times, k0 (2, 0, 2).
Work 14 more rows in established rib patt.
Change to 4 mm (U.S. size 6) needles.
Row 1 K16 (22, 28, 34), work across Row 1 of Panels A, B, C, B, then D, k16 (22, 28, 34).
Row 2 P16 (22, 28, 34), work across Row 2 of Panels D, B, C, B, then A, p16 (22, 28, 34).
Keeping sts before and after cable panels in St st, work 2 more rows in established patt.
Next (dec) row K4, skp, work in patt to last 6 sts, k2tog, k4 – 2 sts dec'd.
Work 9 rows straight.
Rep the last 10 rows 3 more times, then rep dec row once more – 128 (140, 152, 164) sts rem.
Work 1 row straight.

Place pocket linings
Next row K5, place next 34 sts on a holder, work in cable patt across pocket lining sts, work in patt to last 39 sts, place next 34 sts on a holder, work in cable patt across pocket lining sts, k5 – 128 (140, 152, 164) sts.
Work 7 rows straight. Rep dec row – 2 sts dec'd.
Work 9 rows straight.
Rep dec row – 124 (136, 148, 160) sts rem.
Cont same as Back until 7 inc rows for sleeve cap have been worked – 148 (160, 172, 184) sts.
Work 1 row straight.

Shape front neck
Next row (RS) Work in patt 59 (64, 69, 74), turn, leaving rem 89 (96, 103, 110) sts on hold.
Work 1 WS row straight.
Next row K19 (25, 31, 37), M1, work in patt to last 2 sts, work 2 tog – 59 (64, 69, 74) sts rem.
Work 1 WS row straight.
Next row Work in patt to last 2 sts, work 2 tog – 1 st dec'd.
Cont dec 1 st at neck edge every RS row 16 more times, and AT THE SAME TIME cont inc 1 st for sleeve as for back 4 more times, then work 3 (5, 7, 9) rows without inc at armhole edge, ending with a WS row.

Shape upper left sleeve
Cast off 4 sts at beg of every RS row 7 (8, 9, 10) times – 18 (19, 20, 21) sts rem.
Work 1 row straight.

Shape left shoulder
Cast off 9 sts, work in patt to end – 9 (10, 11, 12) sts rem.
Work 1 row straight.
Cast off rem sts.
With RS facing, rejoin yarn to rem sts, cast off next 30 (32, 34, 36) sts, work in patt to end – 59 (64, 69, 74) sts rem.
Work 1 WS row straight.
Next row Work 2 tog, work in patt to last 19 (25, 31, 37) sts, M1, k19 (25, 31, 37) sts – 59 (64, 69, 74) sts.

Work 1 WS row straight.

Next row Work 2 tog, work in patt to end – 1 st dec'd.

Cont dec 1 st at neck edge every RS row 16 more times, and AT THE SAME TIME inc 1 st for sleeve as for back 4 more times – 46 (51, 56, 61) sts rem.

Work 4 (6, 8, 10) rows straight, ending with a RS row.

Shape upper right sleeve

Cast off 4 sts at beg of every WS row 7 (8, 9, 10) times – 18 (19, 20, 21) sts rem.

Work 1 row straight.

Shape right shoulder

Cast off 9 sts, work in patt to end – 9 (10, 11, 12) sts rem.

Work 1 row straight.

Cast off rem sts.

COLLAR

Sew right shoulder and upper arm seam.

With RS facing and using 3.25 mm (U.S. size 3) needles, pick up and k45 sts down left front neck, 32 (34, 35, 37) across front neck, pick up and k45 sts up right front neck, then 42 (43, 45, 46) sts across back neck – 164 (167, 170, 173) sts.

Rib row 1 P2, [k1, p2] to end.

Rib row 2 K2, [p1, k2] to end.

Rep the last 2 rows until collar measures 8 cm (3¼"), ending with Rib Row 1.

Next (inc) row K2, [p1, M1, k2] to end – 218 (222, 226, 230) sts.

Change to 4 mm (U.S. size 6) needles.

Rib row 3 P2 [k2, p2] to end.

Rib row 4 K2 [p2, k2] to end.

Cont in established rib patt for 13 cm (5").

Cast off loosely in rib.

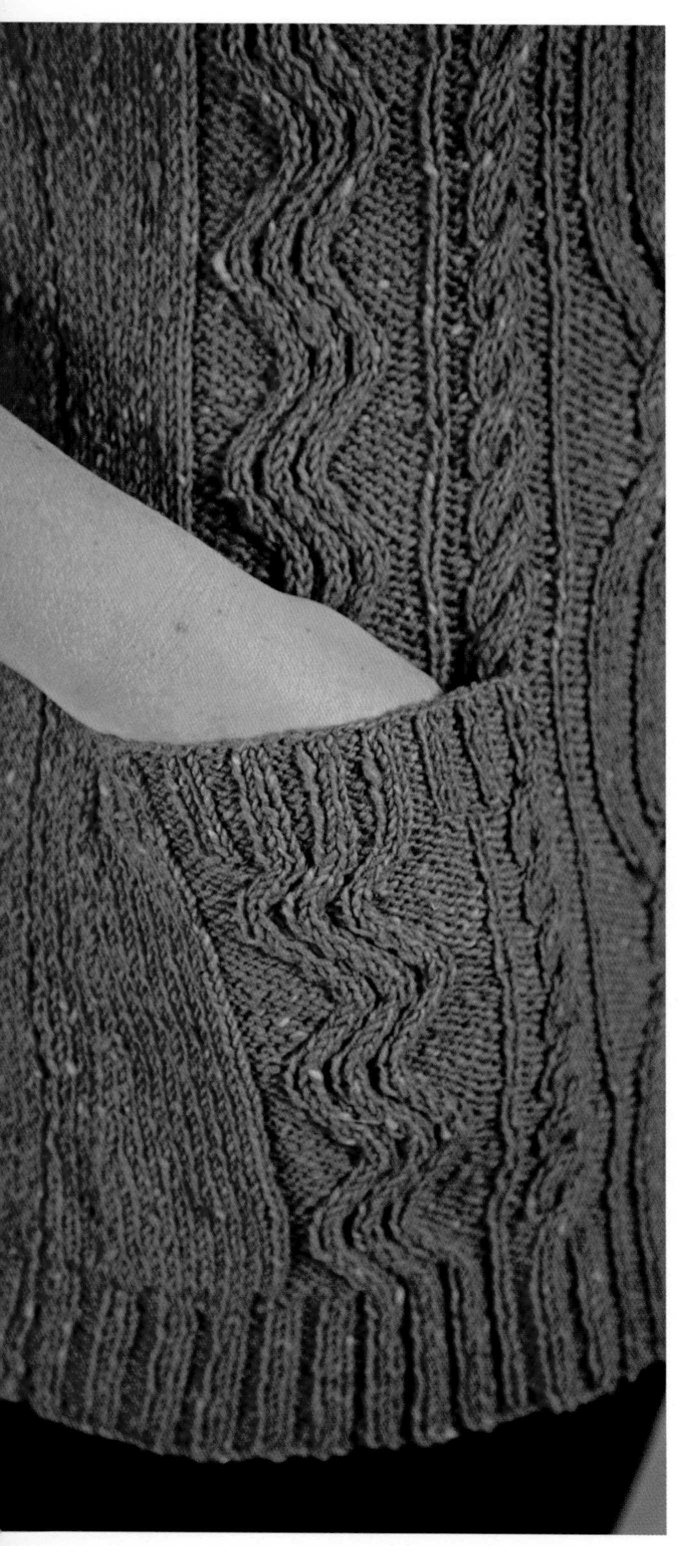

ARMBANDS

Sew left shoulder and collar, reversing seam on last 18 cm (7") of collar.

With RS facing and using 3.25 mm (U.S. size 3) needles, pick up and k110 (114, 118, 122) sts between m.

Rib row 1 P2, [k2, p2] to end.

Rib row 2 K2, [p2, k2] to end.

Rep the last 2 rows 5 more times, then rep Rib Row 1 once more.

Cast off loosely in rib.

POCKET TOPS

With RS facing and using 4 mm (U.S. size 6) needles, work across 34 sts on holder, as foll:

Row 1 (RS) K3, [p2, k2] to last 5 sts, p2, k3.

Row 2 P3, [k2, p2] to last 3 sts, k2, p3.

Rep the last 2 rows once more, then rep Row 1 once more.

Cast off in rib.

MAKING UP

Sew side and armband seams. Block to finished measurements.

Tweed hat

There is a retro feel to this chequerboard pattern and to the soft shape of the hat, knitted in 'Rowan Fine Tweed'. The soft mix of colours go well with most neutrals and give a winter jacket or coat a great shot of colour.

FINISHED SIZE

One size

Brim circumference approx 53.5 cm (21")

YARN

'Rowan Fine Tweed' (100% wool; 90 m [98 yd]/25 g):

1 ball each in Richmond 381 (A), Gunnerside 368 (B), Bainbridge 369 (C), Askrigg 365 (D), Nappa 380 (E), Nidd 382 (F), Hawes 362 (G) and Burnsall 375 (H)

NEEDLES

Pair of 2.75 mm (U.S. size 2) knitting needles

Pair of 3 mm (no exact U.S. equivalent; between U.S. size 2 and 3) knitting needles

Pair of 3.25 mm (U.S. size 3) knitting needles

Adjust needle size if necessary to obtain correct tension.

TENSION

30 sts and 34 rows = 10 cm (4") in patt using 3.25 mm (U.S. size 3) needles.

ABBREVIATIONS

See page 150.

HAT

Using 2.75 mm (U.S. size 2) needles and C, cast on 142 sts.

Rib row 1 (RS) K2, [p2, k2] to end.

Rib row 2 P2, [k2, p2] to end.

Rep the last 2 rows 5 more times, then rep Row 1 once more.

Inc row 1 (WS) P2, k2, [p1, M1, p1, k1, M1, k1] to last 2 sts, k2 – 210 sts.

Change to 3 mm needles. Work in colour patt as foll:

Row 1 (RS) Knit 2A, [1B, 3A] to end.

Row 2 Purl [1A, 3B] to last 2 sts, 1A, 1B.

Row 3 Knit [1A, 3B] to last 2 sts, 1A, 1B.

Row 4 Purl 2A, [1B, 3A] to end.

Rows 5–12 Rep Rows 1–4 twice more.

Change to 3.25 mm (U.S. size 3) needles.

Row 13 (RS) Knit 2C [1D, 3C] to end.

Row 14 Purl [1C, 3D] to last 2 sts, 1C, 1D.

Row 15 Knit [1C, 3D] to last 2 sts, 1C, 1D.

Row 16 Purl 2C, [1D, 3C] to end.

Rows 17–24 Rep Rows 13–16 twice more.

Row 25 (RS) Knit 2E, [1F, 3E] to end.

Row 26 Purl [1E, 3F] to last 2 sts, 1E, 1F.

Row 27 Knit [1E, 3F] to last 2 sts, 1E, 1F.

Row 28 Purl 2E, [1F, 3E] to end.

Rows 29–36 Rep Rows 25–28 twice more.

Change to 3 mm needles.

Row 37 (RS) Knit 2G, [1H, 3G] to end.

Row 38 Purl [1G, 3H] to last 2 sts, 1G, 1H.

Row 39 Knit [1G, 3H] to last 2 sts, 1G, 1H.

Row 40 Purl 2G, [1H, 3G] to end.

Rows 41–48 Rep Rows 37–40 twice more.

Shape top

Cont in A only.

Next (dec) row [K9, k2tog] to last st, k1 – 191 sts rem.

Next row Purl.

Next (dec) row [K8, k2tog] to last st, k1 – 172 sts rem.

Next row Purl.

Next (dec) row [K7, k2tog] to last st, k1 – 153 sts rem.

Next row Purl.

Next (dec) row [K6, k2tog] to last st, k1 – 134 sts rem.

Next row Purl.

Next (dec) row [K5, k2tog] to last st, k1 – 115 sts rem.

Next row Purl.

Next (dec) row [K4, k2tog] to last st, k1 – 96 sts rem.

Next row Purl.

Next (dec) row [K3, k2tog] to last st, k1 –

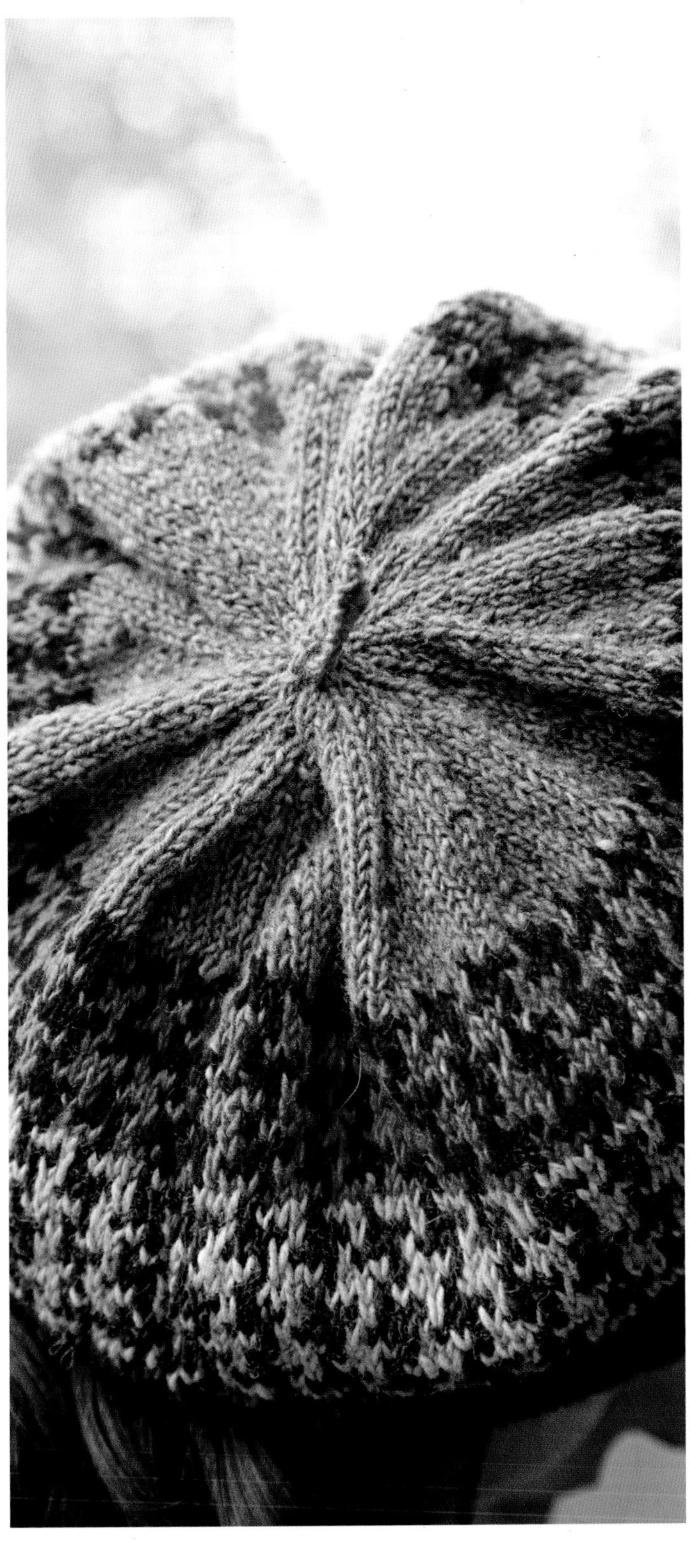

77 sts rem.
Next row Purl.
Next (dec) row [K2, k2tog] to last st, k1 – 58 sts rem.
Next row Purl.
Next (dec) row [K1, k2tog] to last st, k1 – 39 sts rem.
Next row Purl.
Next (dec) row [K2tog] to last st, k1 – 20 sts rem.
Next row Purl.
Next (dec) row K1, [k2tog] to last st, k1 – 11 sts rem.

'STALK'

Using 3.25 mm (U.S. size 3) needles and A, cast on 10 sts.
Knit 2 rows.
Cast off all sts.

MAKING UP

Break yarn and thread through rem sts. Pull up tight and fasten off securely. Sew seam. Sew stalk to centre of hat.

Tweed mittens

Knitted in a classic mitten shape, also in 'Rowan Fine Tweed', these tweed mitts are a great project for practising colourwork, as they won't take too long to knit up.

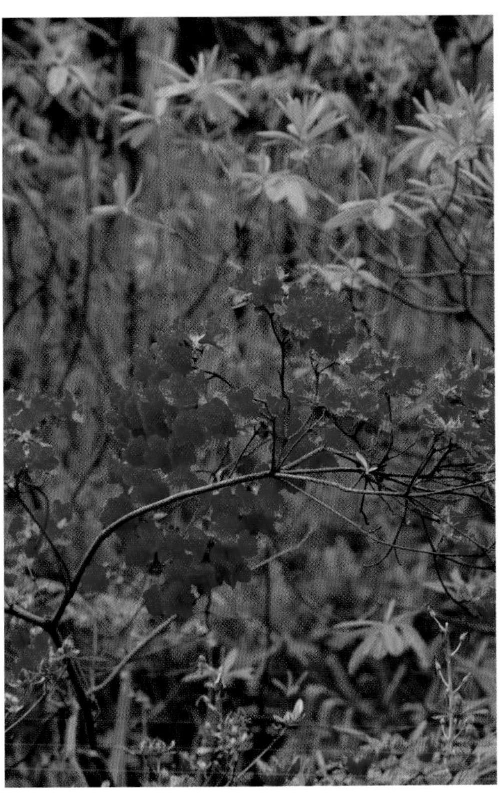

FINISHED SIZE
One size
Hand circumference 18.5 cm (7¼")

YARN
'Rowan Fine Tweed' (100% wool; 90 m [98 yd]/25 g):
1 ball each in Richmond 381 (A), Gunnerside 368 (B), Bainbridge 369 (C), Askrigg 365 (D), Nappa 380 (E), Nidd 382 (F), Hawes 362 (G) and Burnsall 375 (H)

NEEDLES
Pair of 3 mm (no exact U.S. equivalent; between U.S. size 2 and 3) knitting needles
Pair of 3.25 mm (U.S. size 3) knitting needles
Adjust needle size if necessary to obtain correct tension.

EXTRAS
Stitch holder.

TENSION
29 sts and 32 rows = 10 cm (4") in patt using 3.25 mm (U.S. size 3) needles.

STITCH PATTERN
Stripe Pattern (multiple of 4 sts + 2)
Row 1 (RS) Knit 2A, [1B, 3A] to end.
Row 2 Purl [1A, 3B] to last 2 sts, 1A, 1B.
Row 3 Knit [1A, 3B] to last 2 sts, 1A, 1B.
Row 4 Purl 2A, [1B, 3A] to end.
Rows 5–12 Rep Rows 1–4 twice more.
Row 13 (RS) Knit 2C [1D, 3C] to end.
Row 14 Purl [1C, 3D] to last 2 sts, 1C, 1D.
Row 15 Knit [1C, 3D] to last 2 sts, 1C, 1D.

Row 16 Purl 2C, [1D, 3C] to end.
Rows 17–24 Rep Rows 13–16 twice more.
Row 25 (RS) Knit 2E, [1F, 3E] to end.
Row 26 Purl [1E, 3F] to last 2 sts, 1E, 1F.
Row 27 Knit [1E, 3F] to last 2 sts, 1E, 1F.
Row 28 Purl 2E, [1F, 3E] to end.
Rows 29–36 Rep Rows 25–28 twice more.
Row 37 (RS) Knit 2G, [1H, 3G] to end.
Row 38 Purl [1G, 3H] to last 2 sts, 1G, 1H.
Row 39 Knit [1G, 3H] to last 2 sts, 1G, 1H.
Row 40 Purl 2G, [1H, 3G] to end.
Rows 41–48 Rep Rows 37–40 twice more.
Rows 49–60 Rep Rows 1–12.

ABBREVIATIONS

See page 150.

MITTENS (make 2)

Using 3 mm needles and A, cast on 54 sts.
Rib row 1 (RS) K2, [p2, k2] to end.
Rib row 2 P2, [k2, p2] to end.
Rep the last 2 rows 9 more times.
Change to 3.25 mm (U.S. size 3) needles.
Work in Stripe Patt.
AT THE SAME TIME, keeping continuity of Stripe Patt, shape thumb beg on Row 9 as foll:

Thumb shaping

Row 1 (RS) Join separate strand of C, k1, M1, work in established patt to last st, join separate strand of C, M1, k1 – 2 sts inc'd.
Row 2 Using C, p2, work in established patt to last 2 sts, using C, p2.
Row 3 Using C, k2, M1, work in established patt to last 2 sts, using C, M1, k2 – 2 sts inc'd.
Row 4 Using C, p3, work in established patt to last 3 sts, using C, p3.
Row 5 Using C, k3, M1, work in established patt to last 3 sts, using C, M1, k3 – 2 sts inc'd.
Cont inc 1 st each end of every RS row 5 more times – 70 sts.
Next row Using C, p8, turn, leaving rem 62 sts unworked.
Cont in St st on these 8 sts, work 18 rows straight.
Next (dec) row K1, [k2tog] 3 times, k1 – 5 sts rem.
Next (dec) row P1, [p2tog] twice – 2 sts rem.
Cut yarn, leaving a tail about 15 cm (6") long.
Place rem sts on holder.
Return to sts on needle.
Next row Work in patt to last 8 sts, using C, p8.
Next row Using C, k8, turn, leaving rem 54 sts unworked.
Cont in St st on these 8 sts, work 17 rows straight.
Next (dec) row K1, [k2tog] 3 times, k1 – 5 sts rem.
Next (dec) row P1, [p2tog] twice – 2 sts rem.
Cut yarn, leaving a tail about 15 cm (6") long.
Place rem sts on holder.
Return to sts on needle.
Next row Work in patt to end – 54 sts.
Cont in Stripe Patt until 52 rows of patt have been worked from top of rib.

Shape top

Next row Work 27 sts in patt, turn, leaving rem 27 sts unworked. Cont working on these 27 sts.
Cast off 3 sts at beg of next 7 rows – 6 sts rem.
Cast off rem sts.
With RS facing, rejoin yarn to rem 27 sts, work in patt to end.
Cast off 3 sts at beg of next 7 rows – 6 sts rem.
Cast off rem sts.

MAKING UP

Sew top and side seam to base of thumb. Thread an end of yarn through both sets of sts at top of thumb. Pull up tight and fasten off securely. Sew short thumb seam. Sew rem thumb and side seam.

Tweed scarf

This handsome dogstooth check scarf is knitted in four contrasting bands of two different colours of 'Rowan Fine Tweed'. Because it uses only two colours per row, in the Fairisle technique, it is not complicated to knit. This design also comes in a beret and mittens (see pages 102 and 106).

FINISHED SIZE

19.5 cm (7¾") wide and 147.5 cm (58") long

YARN

'Rowan Fine Tweed' (100% wool; 90 m [98 yd]/25 g):
2 balls each in Richmond 381 (A), Gunnerside 368 (B), Bainbridge 369 (C), Askrigg 365 (D), Nappa 380 (E), Nidd 382 (F), Hawes 362 (G) and Burnsall 375 (H)

NEEDLES

Pair of 3.25 mm (U.S. size 3) knitting needles
Adjust needle size if necessary to obtain correct tension.

TENSION

30 sts and 31 rows = 10 cm (4") in patt.

ABBREVIATIONS

See page 150.

SCARF

With A, cast on 122 sts. Work in colour patt as foll:

Row 1 (RS) Knit 2A, [1B, 3A] to end.
Row 2 Purl [1A, 3B] to last 2 sts, 1A, 1B.
Row 3 Knit [1A, 3B] to last 2 sts, 1A, 1B.
Row 4 Purl 2A, [1B, 3A] to end.
Rows 5–12 Rep Rows 1–4 twice more.
Row 13 (RS) Knit 2C, [1D, 3C] to end.
Row 14 Purl [1C, 3D] to last 2 sts, 1C, 1D.
Row 15 Knit [1C, 3D] to last 2 sts, 1C, 1D.
Row 16 Purl 2C, [1D, 3C] to end.
Rows 17–24 Rep Rows 13–16 twice more.
Row 25 (RS) Knit 2E, [1F, 3E] to end.
Row 26 Purl [1E, 3F] to last 2 sts, 1E, 1F.
Row 27 Knit [1E, 3F] to last 2 sts, 1E, 1F.
Row 28 Purl 2E, [1F, 3E] to end.
Rows 29–36 Rep Rows 25–28 twice more.
Row 37 (RS) Knit 2G, [1H, 3G] to end.
Row 38 Purl [1G, 3H] to last 2 sts, 1G, 1H.
Row 39 Knit [1G, 3H] to last 2 sts, 1G, 1H.
Row 40 Purl 2G, [1H, 3G] to end.
Rows 41–48 Rep Rows 37–40 twice more.
Rep Rows 1–48 until piece measures 147.5 cm (58"), ending with Row 12.
With A, cast off.

MAKING UP

Weave in ends. Sew together along side edges.
Centre seam along back of scarf, sew ends.
Block to finished measurements.

Thistle cardigan

This is a neat, cropped cardigan with a Scottish thistle motif on both fronts, while the back and sleeves are worked in graduated stripes in blue and grey. The neckline is slightly scooped. The leaf colour of the thistle pattern is used for the button band, neckband and cuffs. Knitted in 'Rowan Fine Tweed', the thistle pattern is worked using the Fairisle technique.

FINISHED SIZE

To fit bust

81.5	86.5	91.5	96.5	101.5	106.5	112	cm
32	34	36	38	40	42	44	"

ACTUAL MEASUREMENTS

Bust

86.5	92.5	98	103.5	110	115.5	121.5	cm
34	36¼	38½	40¾	43¼	45½	47¾	"

Length to shoulder

47	47.5	49	50	51	52	53.5	cm
18½	18¾	19¼	19¾	20	20½	21	"

Sleeve length 47.5 cm (18¾")

YARN

'Rowan Fine Tweed' (100% wool; 90 m [98 yd]/25 g):

6 (6, 7, 7, 8, 8, 9) balls in Nappa 380 (A)

3 (4, 4, 4, 5, 5, 5) balls in Hubberholme 370 (B)

5 (5, 6, 6, 6, 7, 7) balls in Nidd 382 (C)

NEEDLES

Pair of 2.75 mm (U.S. size 2) knitting needles

Pair of 3.25 mm (U.S. size 3) knitting needles

Adjust needle size if necessary to obtain correct tension.

EXTRAS

Stitch holders; 7 buttons, 15 mm (⅝") Rowan BN1367.

TENSION

28 sts and 38 rows = 10 cm (4") in St st using 3.25 mm (U.S. size 3) needles.

ABBREVIATIONS

See page 150.

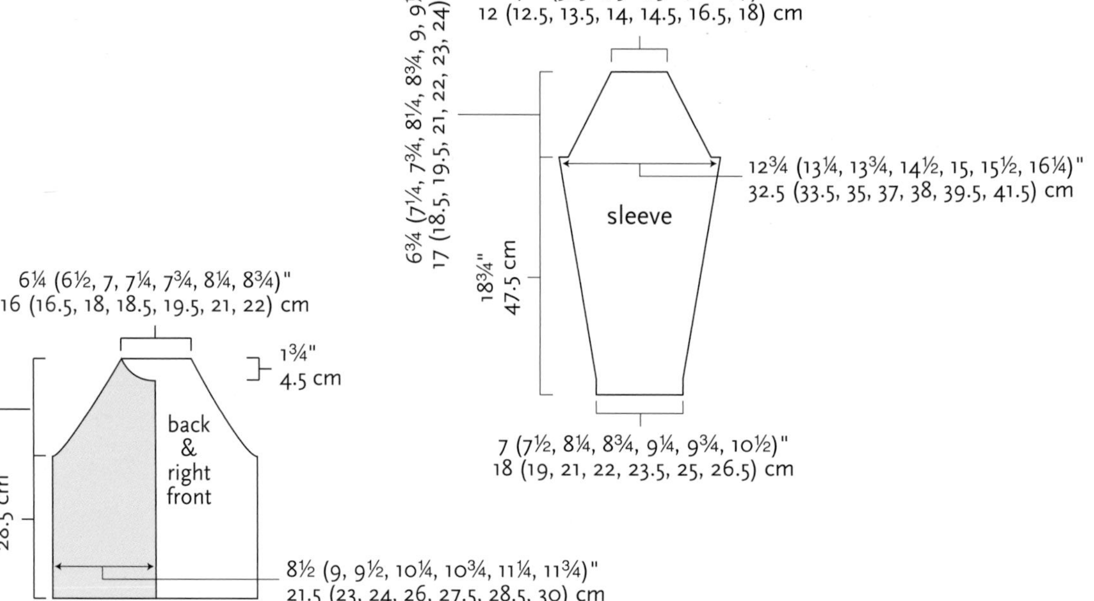

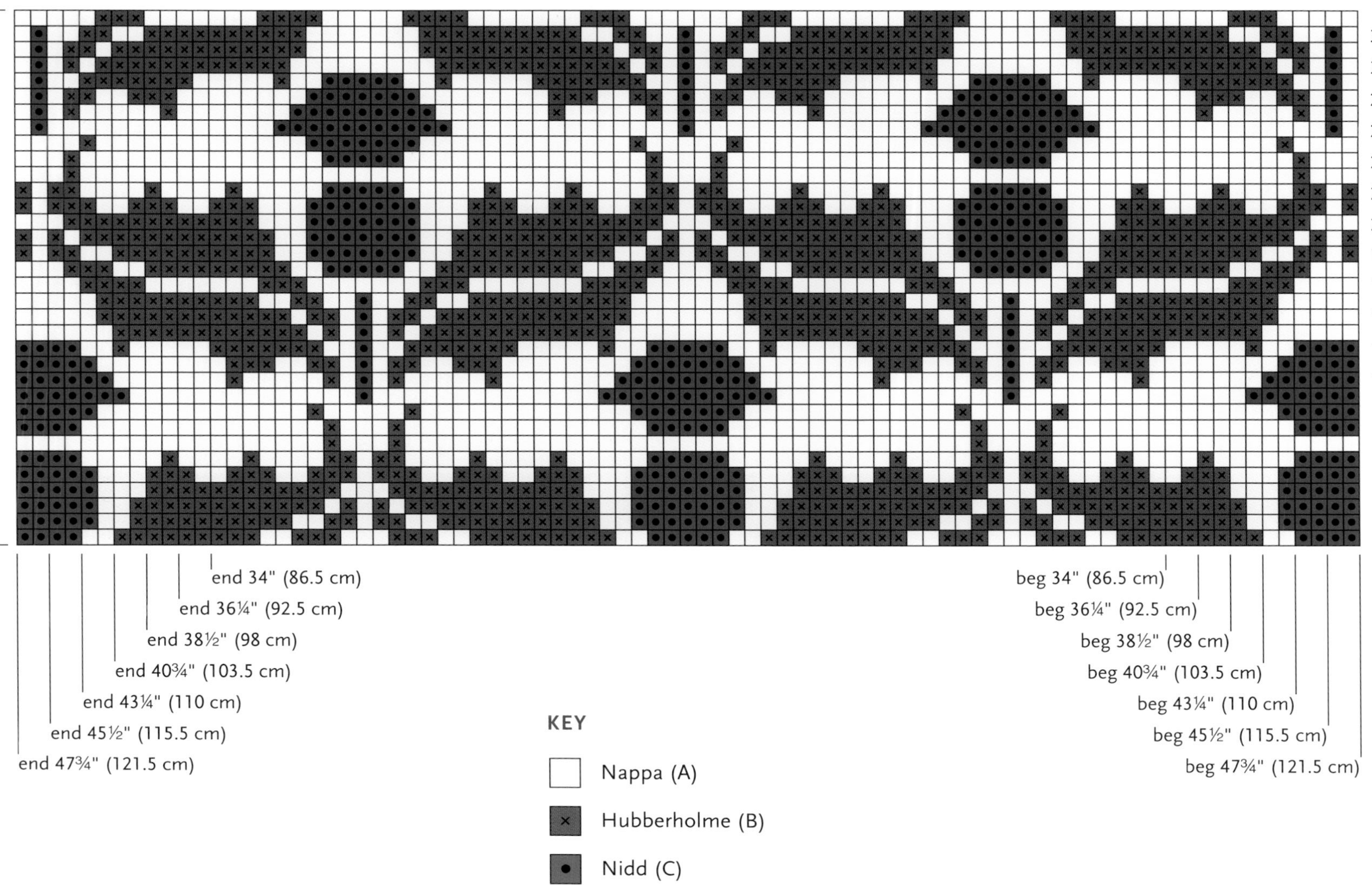

34 row rep
33
31
29
27
25
23
21
19
17
15
13
11
9
7
5
3
1
end 34" (86.5 cm)
end 36¼" (92.5 cm)
end 38½" (98 cm)
end 40¾" (103.5 cm)
end 43¼" (110 cm)
end 45½" (115.5 cm)
end 47¾" (121.5 cm)
beg 34" (86.5 cm)
beg 36¼" (92.5 cm)
beg 38½" (98 cm)
beg 40¾" (103.5 cm)
beg 43¼" (110 cm)
beg 45½" (115.5 cm)
beg 47¾" (121.5 cm)
KEY
Nappa (A)
Hubberholme (B)
Nidd (C)

STRIPE SEQUENCE FOR BACK

[12 rows A, 12 rows C] twice, [8 rows A, 8 rows C] twice, [4 rows A, 4 rows C] 8 times, [2 rows A, 2 rows C] 4 (5, 6, 7, 8, 9, 10) times, 2 rows A – 162 (166, 170, 174, 178, 182, 186) rows.

BACK

Using 2.75 mm (U.S. size 2) needles and B, cast on 119 (127, 135, 143, 151, 159, 167) sts.
Rib row 1 (RS) K1, [p1, k1] to end.
Rib row 2 P1, [k1, p1] to end.
Rep the last 2 rows 5 more times.
Change to 3.25 mm (U.S. size 3) needles.
Beg with a knit row and work in St st and stripes until 94 rows have been worked, ending with a WS row and 2 rows of C.

Shape raglan armholes

Cast off 5 (6, 6, 7, 7, 8, 8) sts at beg of next 2 rows – 109 (115, 123, 129, 137, 143, 151) sts rem.
Next row (RS) K2, skp, work in patt to last 4 sts, k2tog, k2 – 2 sts dec'd.
Work 1 WS row straight.
Rep the last 2 rows 32 (34, 36, 38, 40, 42, 44) more times – 43 (45, 49, 51, 55, 57, 61) sts rem.
Place rem sts on a holder.

LEFT FRONT

Using 2.75 mm (U.S. size 2) needles and B, cast on 59 (63, 67, 71, 75, 79, 83) sts.
Rib row 1 (RS) P1, [k1, p1] to end.
Rib row 2 K1, [p1, k1] to end.
Rep the last 2 rows 5 more times.
Change to 3.25 mm (U.S. size 3) needles.
Beg with a knit row and work in St st from chart until 94 rows have been worked, ending with a WS row and 2 rows of C.

Shape armhole

Next row Cast off 5 (6, 6, 7, 7, 8, 8) sts, work in patt to end – 54 (57, 61, 64, 68, 71, 75) sts rem.

Work 1 WS row straight.

Next row Skp, work in patt to end – 1 st dec'd.

Work 1 WS row straight.

Rep the last 2 rows 24 (26, 28, 30, 32, 34, 36) more times – 29 (30, 32, 33, 35, 36, 38) sts rem.

Shape neck

Next row (RS) Skp, work 14 sts in established patt, k2tog, turn and place rem 11 (12, 14, 15, 17, 18, 20) sts on a holder – 16 sts rem in work.

Work 1 WS row straight.

Next row Skp, work in patt to last 2 sts, k2tog – 2 sts dec'd.

Rep the last 2 rows 6 more times – 2 sts rem.

Work 1 WS row straight.

Place rem sts on a small st holder or safety pin.

RIGHT FRONT

Using 2.75 mm (U.S. size 2) needles and B, cast on 59 (63, 67, 71, 75, 79, 83) sts.

Rib row 1 (RS) P1, [k1, p1] to end.

Rib row 2 K1, [p1, k1] to end.

Rep the last 2 rows 5 more times.

Change to 3.25 mm (U.S. size 3) needles.

Beg with a knit row and work in St st from chart until 95 rows have been worked, ending with a RS row and 3 rows of C.

Shape armhole

Next row Cast off 5 (6, 6, 7, 7, 8, 8) sts, work in patt to end – 54 (57, 61, 64, 68, 71, 75) sts rem.

Next row Work in patt to last 2 sts, k2tog – 1 st dec'd.

Work 1 WS row straight.

Rep the last 2 rows 24 (26, 28, 30, 32, 34, 36) more times – 29 (30, 32, 33, 35, 36, 38) sts rem.

Cut A and C.

Shape neck

Next row Using B, k11 (12, 14, 15, 17, 18, 20), place sts on a holder, rejoin A and C, skp, work in established patt to last 2 sts, k2tog – 2 sts dec'd.

Work 1 WS row straight.

Next row Skp, work in patt to last 2 sts, k2tog – 1 st dec'd.

Rep the last 2 rows 6 more times – 2 sts rem.

Work 1 WS row straight.

Place rem sts on a small st holder or safety pin.

STRIPE SEQUENCE FOR SLEEVES

[12 rows A, 12 rows C] 5 times, [8 rows A, 8 rows C] twice, [4 rows A, 4 rows C] 8 times, [2 rows A, 2 rows C] 4 (5, 6, 7, 8, 9, 10) times, 2 rows A – 234 (238, 242, 246, 250, 254, 258) rows.

SLEEVES

Using 2.75 mm (U.S. size 2) needles and B, cast on 49 (53, 57, 61, 65, 69, 73) sts.

Rib row 1 (RS) P1, [k1, p1] to end.

Rib row 2 K1, [p1, k1] to end.

Rep the last 2 rows 5 more times.

Change to 3.25 mm (U.S. size 3) needles.

Beg with a knit row cont in St st and stripes.

Work 2 rows.

Inc row K3, M1, knit to last 3 sts, M1, k3 – 2 sts inc'd.

Work 7 rows straight.

Rep the last 8 rows 18 more times, then rep

inc row once more – 89 (93, 97, 101, 105, 109, 113) sts.
Work straight until 166 rows of stripe patt have been worked, ending with a WS row.

Shape raglans
Cast off 5 (6, 6, 7, 7, 8, 8) sts at beg of next 2 rows – 79 (81, 85, 87, 91, 93, 97) sts rem.
Sizes 110 (115.5, 121.5) cm (43¼ [45½, 47¾]") only
Next row K2, skp, knit to last 4 sts, k2tog, k2 – 2 sts dec'd.
Work 5 rows straight.
Rep the last 6 rows 1 (3, 5) more time(s) – 87 (85, 85) sts rem.
All sizes
Next row K2, skp, knit to last 4 sts, k2tog, k2 – 2 sts dec'd.
Work 3 rows straight.
Rep the last 4 rows 7 (9, 11, 13, 11, 9, 7) more times – 63 (61, 61, 59, 63, 65, 69) sts rem.
Next row K2, skp, knit to last 4 sts, k2tog, k2 – 2 sts dec'd.
Work 1 row straight.
Rep the last 2 rows 14 (13, 11, 9, 10, 9, 9) more times – 33 (35, 37, 39, 41, 45, 49) sts rem.
Work 4 (2, 2, 2, 0, 2, 2) rows straight.
Place rem sts on a spare needle.

NECKBAND

With RS facing, using 2.75 mm (U.S. size 2) needles and B, k11 (12, 14, 15, 17, 18, 20) sts from right front holder, pick up and k15 sts along front neck, k1 from right front holder, then knit next st from holder tog with first st of right sleeve, k31 (33, 35, 37, 39, 43, 47) sleeve sts, knit last sleeve st tog with first st on back, k41 (43, 47, 49, 53, 55, 59) back sts, knit last back st tog with first st of right sleeve, k31 (33, 35, 37, 39, 43, 47) sleeve sts, knit last sleeve st tog with first st on left front holder, k1, pick up and k15 sts along left side of front neck, k11 (12, 14, 15, 17, 18, 20) sts from left front holder – 161 (169, 181, 189, 201, 213, 229) sts.
Rib row 1 K1, [p1, k1] to end.
Rib row 2 P1, [k1, p1] to end.
Rep the last 2 rows 3 more times, then rep Row 1 once more.
Cast off in rib.

BUTTON BAND

With RS facing, using 2.75 mm (U.S. size 2) needles and B, pick up and k125 (127, 129, 131, 133, 135, 137) sts down left front.
Rib row 1 K1, [p1, k1] to end.
Rib row 2 P1, [k1, p1] to end.
Rep the last 2 rows 3 more times, then rep Row 1 once more.
Cast off in rib.

BUTTONHOLE BAND

With RS facing, using 2.75 mm (U.S. size 2) needles and B, pick up and k125 (127, 129, 131, 133, 135, 137) sts up right front.
Rib row 1 K1, [p1, k1] to end.
Rib row 2 P1, [k1, p1] to end.
Rep the last 2 rows once more.
Buttonhole row Work 4 (5, 6, 4, 5, 6, 4) in established rib patt, [k2tog or p2tog to maintain patt, yrn, work next 17 (17, 17, 18, 18, 18, 19) sts in established rib patt] 6 times, k2tog or p2tog to maintain patt, yrn, work rem 5 (6, 7, 5, 6, 7, 5) sts in established rib patt.
Work 4 rows straight in established rib patt.
Cast off in rib.

MAKING UP

Sew raglan seams. Sew side and sleeve seams. Sew underarm seams. Sew on buttons.

Braemar waistcoat

This easy-to-wear cap-sleeved waistcoat cum shrug is knitted in 'Rowan Fine Tweed' in a simple stripe pattern in five colours, using one of them to create the deep ribbed hem, buttonband and belt, and to trim the sleeves. The waistcoat finishes just below the waist, with four buttons on the ribbed part.

FINISHED SIZE

S	M	L	XL	
To fit bust				
81.5–86.5	91.5–96.5	101.5–106.5	112–117	cm
32–34	36–38	40–42	44–46	"

ACTUAL MEASUREMENTS

Bust				
96.5	108	119.5	131	cm
38	42½	47	51½	"
Length to shoulder				
53.5	54.5	55	56	cm
21	21½	21¾	22	"

YARN

'Rowan Fine Tweed' (100% wool; 90 m [98 yd]/25 g):
7 (8, 8, 9) balls in Burnsall 375 (A)
2 (3, 3, 4) balls each in Skipton 379 (B), Hawes 362 (C), Richmond 381 (D) and Leyburn 383 (E)

NEEDLES

Pair of 2.75 mm (U.S. size 2) knitting needles
Pair of 3.25 mm (U.S. size 3) knitting needles
Adjust needle size if necessary to obtain correct tension.

EXTRAS

Locking marker (m); 4 buttons, 2 cm (¾") Rowan BN1367.

TENSION

28 sts and 44 rows = 10 cm (4") in patt using 3.25 mm (U.S. size 3) needles.

ABBREVIATIONS

See page 150.

BACK

Using 2.75 mm (U.S. size 2) needles and A, cast on 117 (133, 149, 165) sts.
Rib row 1 (RS) K1, [p1, k1] to end.
Rib row 2 P1, [k1, p1] to end.
Rep the last 2 rows 25 more times. Rib should measure about 13.5 cm (5¼") from cast on.
Change to 3.25 mm (U.S. size 3) needles.
Work in patt and stripe sequence as foll:
2 rows each A, B, C, D, then E.
Row 1 (RS) Using A, k1, [sl 1 purlwise wyif, k1] to end.
Row 2 Using A, purl.
Rep Rows 1 and 2, and stripe sequence.

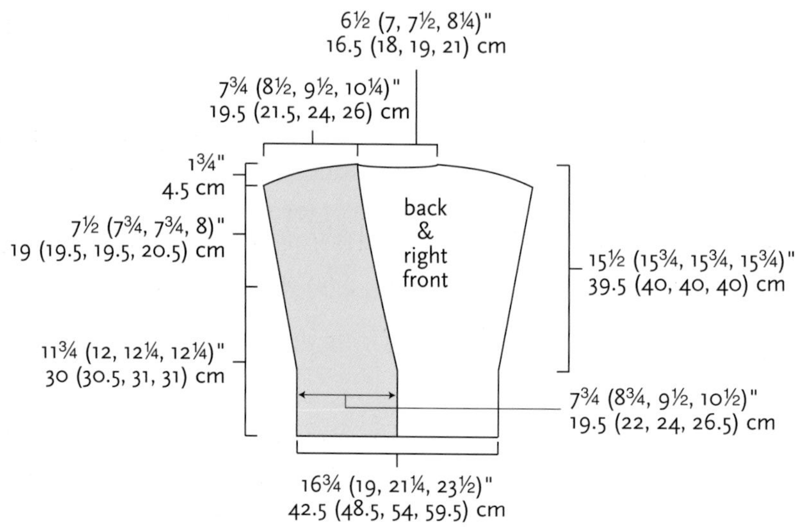

Work 2 (4, 6, 8) rows.

Inc 1 st each end of the next row, then every 8 rows 8 more times – 135 (151, 167, 183) sts. Work new sts in patt.

Work 3 rows straight. Piece should measure about 30 (30.5, 31, 31) cm (11¾ [12, 12¼, 12¼]") from cast on.

Place marker (pm) at each end of last row to mark beg of armhole.

Work 4 rows straight.

Inc 1 st each end of the next row, then every 8 rows 8 more times – 153 (169, 185, 201) sts.

Work 13 (15, 17, 19) rows straight, ending with a WS row. Piece should measure about 49 (50, 51, 51.5) cm (19¼ [19¾, 20, 20¼]") from cast on.

Shape upper arm

Cast off 4 sts at beg of next 8 rows, then 4 (5, 6, 7) sts at beg of next 8 rows – 89 (97, 105, 113) sts rem.

Shape shoulders and back neck

Next row (RS) Cast off 11 (12, 13, 14) sts, work in established patt until there are 14 (16, 18, 20) sts on right needle, turn, leaving rem 64 (69, 74, 79) sts on hold.

Next row Cast off 3 (4, 5, 6) sts, work in patt to end – 11 (12, 13, 14) sts rem.

Cast off rem sts.

With RS facing, rejoin yarn to rem sts, cast off the next 39 (41, 43, 45) sts, work in patt to end – 25 (28, 31, 34) sts rem.

Next row Cast off 11 (12, 13, 14) sts, work in patt to end – 14 (16, 18, 20) sts rem.

Next row Cast off 3 (4, 5, 6) sts, work in patt to end – 11 (12, 13, 14) sts rem.

Cast off rem sts.

LEFT FRONT

Using 2.75 mm (U.S. size 2) needles and A, cast on 55 (61, 67, 73) sts.

Rib row 1 (RS) P1, [k1, p1] to end.

Rib row 2 K1, [p1, k1] to end.

Rep the last 2 rows 25 more times. Rib should measure about 13.5 cm (5¼") from cast on.

Change to 3.25 mm (U.S. size 3) needles.

Work in patt and stripe sequence as foll:

2 rows each A, B, C, D, then E.

Row 1 (RS) Using A, k1, [sl 1 purlwise wyif, k1] to end.

Row 2 Using A, purl.

Rep Rows 1 and 2, and stripe sequence.

Work 2 (4, 6, 8) rows.

Next (shaping) row (RS) K1, M1, work in established patt to last 2 sts, k2tog – 55 (61, 67, 73) sts. Work new st in patt.

Work 7 rows straight.

Rep the last 8 rows 7 more times, then rep the shaping row once more – 55 (61, 67, 73) sts.

Work 3 rows straight. Piece should measure about 30 (30.5, 31, 31) cm (11¾ [12, 12¼, 12¼]") from cast on.

Pm at end of last row to mark beg of armhole.

Work 4 rows straight.

Rep shaping row on next row, then every 8 rows 7 more times, then rep shaping row once more – 55 (61, 67, 73) sts.

Work 7 rows straight.

Next (dec) row (RS) Work in patt to last 2 sts, k2tog – 54 (60, 66, 72) sts rem.

Work 5 (7, 9, 11) rows straight, ending with a WS row. Piece should measure about 49 (50, 51, 51.5) cm (19¼ [19¾, 20, 20¼]") from cast on.

Shape upper arm

Cast off at beg of RS rows 4 sts 4 times, then 4 (5, 6, 7) sts 4 times – 22 (24, 26, 28) sts rem.

Work 1 row straight.

Shape shoulder

Next row Cast off 11 (12, 13, 14) sts, work in patt to end – 11 (12, 13, 14) sts rem.

Work 1 row straight.

Cast off rem sts.

RIGHT FRONT

Using 2.75 mm (U.S. size 2) needles and A, cast on 55 (61, 67, 73) sts.

Rib row 1 P1, [k1, p1] to end.

Rib row 2 K1, [p1, k1] to end.

Rep the last 2 rows 25 more times. Piece should measure about 13.5 cm (5¼") from cast on.

Change to 3.25 mm (U.S. size 3) needles.

Work in patt and stripe sequence as foll: 2 rows each A, B, C, D, then E.

Row 1 (RS) Using A, k1, [sl 1 purlwise wyif, k1] to end.

Row 2 Using A, purl.

Rep Rows 1 and 2, and stripe sequence.

Work 2 (4, 6, 8) rows.

Next (shaping) row (RS) K2tog, work in established patt to last st, M1, k1 – 55 (61, 67, 73) sts.

Work 7 rows straight.

Rep the last 8 rows 7 more times then rep the shaping row once more – 55 (61, 67, 73) sts.

Work 3 rows straight, ending with a WS row. Piece should measure about 30 (30.5, 31, 31) cm (11¾ [12, 12¼, 12¼]") from cast on.

Pm at beg of last row to mark beg of armhole.

Work 4 rows straight.

Rep shaping row on next row, then every 8 rows 7 more times, then rep the shaping row once more – 55 (61, 67, 73) sts.

Work 7 rows straight.

Next (dec) row (RS) K2tog, work in patt to end – 54 (60, 66, 72) sts rem.

Work 6 (8, 10, 12) rows straight, ending with a RS row. Piece should measure about 49 (50, 51, 51.5) cm (19¼ [19¾, 20, 20¼]") from cast on.

Shape upper arm

Cast off at beg of WS rows 4 sts time, then 4 (5, 6, 7) sts 4 times – 22 (24, 26, 28) sts rem.
Work 1 row straight.

Shape shoulder

Next row Cast off 11 (12, 13, 14) sts, work in patt to end – 11 (12, 13, 14) sts rem.
Work 1 row straight.
Cast off rem sts.
Weave in ends. Block pieces to finished measurements.

BUTTON BAND

Sew shoulder seams.
Pm at centre of back neck.
With RS facing, using 2.75 mm (U.S. size 2) needles and A, beg at m and pick up and k22 (24, 26, 28) sts along back neck to shoulder, 131 (133, 135, 137) sts along left front to top of rib, and 39 sts along edge of rib – 192 (196, 200, 204) sts.
Row 1 (WS) [K 1, p1] to end.
Rep the last row 7 more times.
Cast off loosely in rib.

BUTTONHOLE BAND

With RS facing, using 2.75 mm (U.S. size 2) needles and A, beg at bottom of right front and, pick up and k39 sts along edge of rib, 131 (133, 135, 137) sts along right front to shoulder, and 22 (24, 26, 28) sts along back neck to m – 192 (196, 200, 204) sts.
Row 1 (WS) [K 1, p1] to end.
Rep the last row 2 more times.
Buttonhole row Work 3 sts in established rib, yrn, k2tog, [work 10 sts in rib, yrn, k2tog] 3 times, work rib to end.
Work 4 rows straight.
Cast off loosely in rib.

ARMBANDS

With RS facing, using 2.75 mm (U.S. size 2) needles and A, pick up and k130 (134, 138, 142) sts evenly between m.
Row 1 (WS) [K 1, p1] to end.
Rep the last row 7 more times.
Cast off loosely in rib.

BELT

Using 2.75 mm (U.S. size 2) needles and A, cast on 13 sts.
Rib row 1 K2, [p1, k1] to last 3 sts, p1, k2.
Rib row 2 K1, [p1, k1] to end.
Rep the last 2 rows until belt measures 190.5 (200.5, 211, 221)cm (75 [79, 83, 87]") from cast on.
Cast off in rib.

BELT CARRIERS (make 6)

Using 2.75 mm (U.S. size 2) needles and A, cast on 7 sts.
Rib row 1 K2, p1, k1, p1, k2.
Rib row 2 K1, [p1, k1] to end.
Rep the last 2 rows 6 more times.
Cast off in rib.

MAKING UP

Sew button band to buttonhole band at back neck. Sew side and armband seams. Sew on belt carriers using photo as guide. Sew on buttons.

Braemar scarf

Knitted in the same yarn and stripe pattern as the Braemar waistcoat, this scarf rings the colour changes with a palette of primarily soft rust, gold and green. It makes a great introduction to simple knitting in colour. With its close stripes, the yarn is carried up the scarf at the sides – no need to weave in ends.

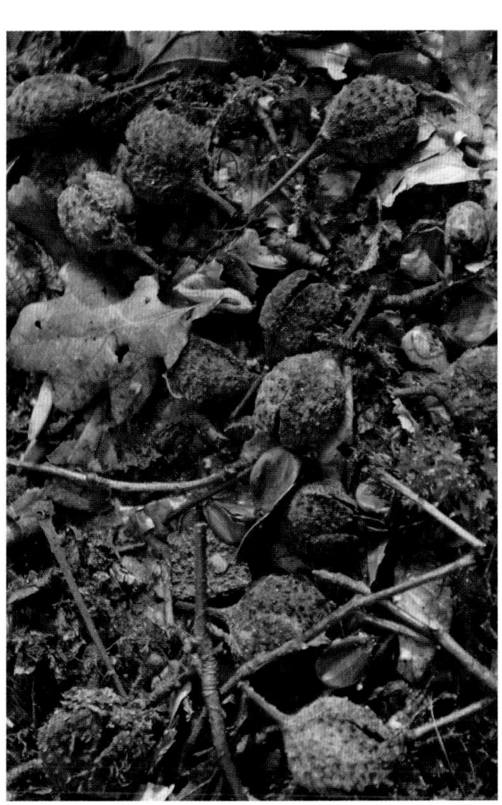

FINISHED SIZE
20.5 cm (8") wide and 154.5 cm (60¾") long

YARN
'Rowan Fine Tweed' (100% wool; 90 m [98 yd]/25 g):
2 balls each in Gunnerside 368 (A), Leyburn 383 (B), Hubberholme 370 (C), Buckden 364 (D) and Bainbridge 369 (E)

NEEDLES
Pair of 3.25 mm (U.S. size 3) knitting needles
Adjust needle size if necessary to obtain correct tension.

TENSION
30 sts and 48 rows = 10 cm (4") in patt.

ABBREVIATIONS
See page 150.

NOTE
Slip stitches purlwise.

SCARF
With A, cast on 61 sts.
Work in patt and stripe sequence as foll:
Row 1 (RS) With A, k1, [sl 1 wyif, k1] to end.
Row 2 With A, purl.
Rows 3 and 4 With B, rep Rows 1 and 2.
Rows 5 and 6 With C, rep Rows 1 and 2.
Rows 7 and 8 With D, rep Rows 1 and 2.
Rows 9 and 10 With E, rep Rows 1 and 2.
Rep Rows 1–10 until piece measures 154.5 cm (60¾"), ending with a purl row.
Cast off knitwise with last colour used.

Fyfe cardigan

This classic crop-sleeved cardigan in 'Rowan Tweed', is ideal for layering over finer tops or a cotton dress. It offers a great opportunity to practise textured knitting, with its beautifully worked cables, and makes a cosy but structured garment with natural elegance.

FINISHED SIZE

S	M	L	XL	
To fit bust				
81.5–86.5	91.5–96.5	101.5–106.5	112–117	cm
32–34	36–38	40–42	44–46	"

ACTUAL MEASUREMENTS

Bust				
98	112	124.5	134.5	cm
39	44	49	53	"
Length to shoulder				
58	59	61	62	cm
22¾	23¼	24	24½	"

YARN

8 (9, 10, 10) balls of 'Rowan Tweed' (100% wool; 118 m [129 yd]/50 g) in Bainbridge 588

NEEDLES

Pair of 3.25 mm (U.S. size 3) knitting needles
Pair of 4 mm (U.S. size 6) knitting needles
Adjust needle size if necessary to obtain correct tension.

EXTRAS

Cable needle (cn); locking markers (m); 5 buttons, 2 cm (¾") Rowan BN1367

TENSION

20 sts and 32 rows = 10 cm (4") in Moss st using 4 mm (U.S. size 6) needles; 15 sts of cable panel = 5 cm (2") wide.

ABBREVIATIONS

K1tbl: knit one st through back of loop.
C6B: slip next 3 sts onto cn and hold in back of work, k3 then k3 from cn.
C7B: slip next 4 sts onto cn and hold in back of work, k3 then k4 from cn.
C4R: slip next stitch onto cn and hold in back of work, k3, then k1 from cn.
C4L: slip next 3 sts onto cn and hold in front of work, k1, then k3 from cn.
T4R: slip next stitch onto cn and hold in back of work, k3, then p1 from cn.
T4L: slip next 3 sts onto cn and hold in front of work, p1, then k3 from cn.
See also page 150.

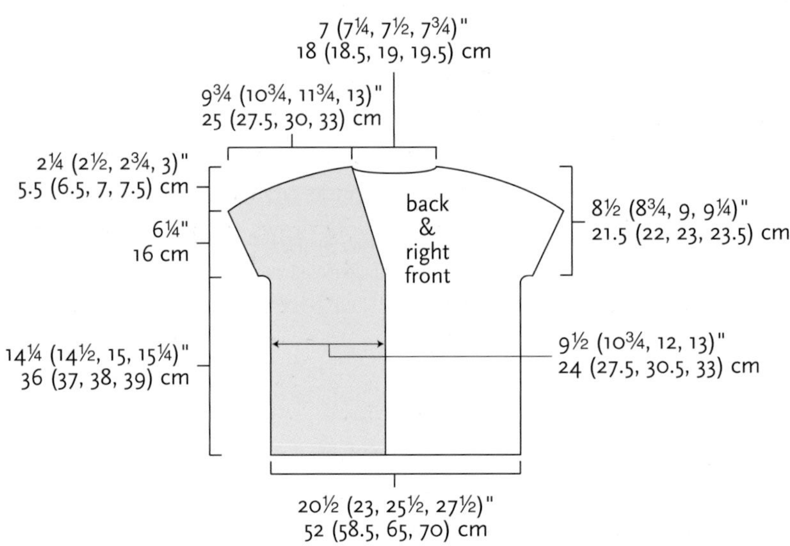

CABLE PANEL (15 sts)
Row 1 (RS) P3, C4R, p1, C4L, p3.
Row 2 K3, p4, k1, p4, k3.
Row 3 P2, C4R, p1, k1, p1, C4L, p2.
Row 4 K2, p4, k1, p1, k1, p4, k2.
Row 5 P1, C4R, [p1, k1] twice, p1, C4L, p1.
Row 6 K1, p4, [k1, p1] twice, k1, p4, k1.
Row 7 C4R, [p1, k1] 3 times, p1, C4L.
Row 8 P4, [k1, p1] 3 times, k1, p4.
Row 9 K3, [p1, k1] 4 times, p1, k3.
Row 10 P3, [k1, p1] 4 times, k1, p3.
Row 11 T4L, [p1, k1] 3 times, p1, T4R.
Row 12 K1, p3, [k1, p1] 3 times, p3, k1.
Row 13 P1, T4L, [p1, k1] twice, p1, T4R, p1.
Row 14 K2, p3, [k1, p1] twice, k1, p3, k2.
Row 15 P2, T4L, p1, k1, p1, T4R, p2.
Row 16 K3, p3, k1, p1, k1, p3, k3.
Row 17 P3, T4L, p1, T4R, p3.
Row 18 K4, p3, k1, p3, k4.
Row 19 P4, C7B, p4.
Row 20 K4, p7, k4.
Rep Rows 1–20 for patt.

BACK

Using 3.25 mm (U.S. size 3) needles, cast on 136 (148, 160, 172) sts.
Row 1 (RS) [K1tbl, p1] 7 (10, 13, 16) times, *k6, p1, [k1tbl, p1] 5 times; rep from * 5 more times, k6, [p1, k1tbl] 7 (10, 13, 16) times.
Row 2 [P1, k1] 7 (10, 13, 16) times, *p6, k1, [p1, k1] 5 times; rep from * 5 more times, p6, [k1, p1] 7 (10, 13, 16) times.
Row 3 [K1tbl, p1] 7 (10, 13, 16) times, *C6B, p1, [k1tbl, p1] 5 times; rep from * 5 more times, C6B, [p1, k1tbl] 7 (10, 13, 16) times.
Row 4 Rep Row 2.
Rows 5–32 Rep Rows 1–4 seven more times.
Row 33 [K1tbl, p1] 7 (10, 13, 16) times, *k6, p1, [k1tbl, p1] 5 times, k3, M1, k3, p1, [k1tbl, p1] 5 times; rep from * twice more, k6, [p1, k1tbl] 7 (10, 13, 16) times – 139 (151, 163, 175) sts.
Row 34 [P1, k1] 7 (10, 13, 16) times, *p6, k1, [p1, k1] 5 times, p7, k1, [p1, k1] 5 times; rep from * twice more, p6, [k1, p1] 7 (10, 13, 16) times.
Change to 4 mm (U.S. size 6) needles.
Work in patt as foll:
Row 1 (RS) [K1, p1] 5 (8, 11, 14) times, [k1tbl, p3, C6B, p3, k1tbl, p3, work Row 19 of Cable Panel, p3] 3 times, k1tbl, p3, C6B, p3, k1tbl, [p1, k1] 5 (8, 11 ,14) times.
Row 2 [K1, p1] 5 (8, 11, 14) times, [p1, k3, p6, k3, p1, k3, work Row 20 of Cable Panel, k3] 3 times, p1, k3, p6, k3, p1, [p1, k1] 5 (8, 11, 14) times.
Row 3 [K1, p1] 5 (8, 11, 14) times, [k1tbl, p3, k6, p3, k1tbl, p3, work Row 1 of Cable Panel, p3] 3 times, k1tbl, p3, k6, p3, k1tbl, [p1, k1] 5 (8, 11, 14) times.
Row 4 [K1, p1] 5 (8, 11, 14) times, [p1, k3, p6, k3, p1, k3, work Row 2 of Cable Panel, k3] 3 times, p1, k3, p6, k3, p1, [p1, k1] 5 (8, 11, 14) times.
Cont in established patt until piece measures 36 (37, 38, 39) cm (14¼ [14½, 15, 15¼]") from cast on, ending with a WS row.
Place locking m at each end of last row to mark beg of armhole.

Shape cap sleeves

Row 1 Work 10 (16, 22, 28) sts in Moss st, M1, work in patt to last 10 (16, 22, 28) sts, M1, work to end – 2 sts inc'd.
Rows 2–4 Work 3 rows straight, working new sts in Moss st.
Row 5 Work 11 (17, 23, 29) sts in Moss st, M1, work in patt to last 11 (17, 23, 29) sts, M1, work to end – 2 sts inc'd.
Rows 6–8 Work 3 rows straight.
Row 9 Work 12 (18, 24, 30) sts in Moss st, M1, work in patt to last 12 (18, 24, 30) sts, M1, work to end – 2 sts inc'd.

Rows 10–12 Work 3 rows straight.
Rep inc row on next row, then every 4 rows 8 more times – 163 (175, 187, 199) sts.
Work 5 rows straight.

Shape upper sleeve
Cast off 4 sts at beg of next 14 (16, 18, 20) rows – 107 (111, 115, 119) sts rem.

Shape shoulders and back neck
Cast off 10 (11, 12, 13) sts at beg of next 2 rows – 87 (89, 91, 93) sts rem.
Next row Cast off 10 sts, work in patt until there are 13 sts on right needle, turn, leaving rem 64 (66, 68, 70) sts on hold.
Next row Cast off 3 sts, work in patt to end – 10 sts rem.
Cast off rem sts.
With RS facing, rejoin yarn to rem 64 (66, 68, 70) sts, cast off next 41 (43, 45, 47) sts, work in patt to end – 23 sts rem.
Next row Cast ff 10 sts, work in patt to end – 13 sts rem.
Next row Cast off 3 sts, work in patt to end – 10 sts rem.
Cast off rem sts.

LEFT FRONT

Using 3.25 mm (U.S. size 3) needles, cast on 59 (65, 71, 77) sts.
Row 1 (RS) [K1tbl, p1] 7 (10, 13, 16) times, *k6, p1, [k1tbl, p1] 5 times; rep from * once more, k6, [p1, k1tbl] twice, p1.
Row 2 K1, [p1, k1] twice, *p6, k1, [p1, k1] 5 times; rep from * once more, p6, [k1, p1] 7 (10, 13, 16) times.
Row 3 [K1tbl, p1] 7 (10, 13, 16) times, *C6B, p1, [k1tbl, p1] 5 times; rep from * once more, C6B, [p1, k1tbl] twice, p1.
Row 4 Rep Row 2.
Rows 5–32 Rep Rows 1–4 seven more times.
Row 33 [K1tbl, p1] 7 (10, 13, 16) times, k6, p1, [k1tbl, p1] 5 times, k3, M1, k3, p1, [k1tbl, p1] 5 times, k6, [p1, k1tbl] twice, p1 – 60 (66, 72, 78) sts.
Row 34 K1, [p1, k1] twice, p6, k1, [p1, k1] 5 times, p7, k1, [p1, k1] 5 times, p6, [k1, p1] 7 (10, 13, 16) times.
Change to 4 mm (U.S. size 6) needles.
Work in patt as foll:
Row 1 (RS) [K1, p1] 5 (8, 11, 14) times, k1tbl, p3, C6B, p3, k1tbl, p3, work Row 19 of Cable Panel, p3, k1tbl, p3, C6B, p3, k1tbl, p1.
Row 2 K1, p1, k3, p6, k3, p1, k3, work Row 20 of Cable Panel, k3, p1, k3, p6, k3, p1, [p1, k1] 5 (8, 11, 14) times.
Row 3 [K1, p1] 5 (8, 11, 14) times, k1tbl, p3, k6, p3, k1tbl, p3, work Row 1 of Cable Panel, p3, k1tbl, p3, k6, p3, k1tbl, p1.
Row 4 K1, p1, k3, p6, k3, p1, k3, work Row 2 of Cable Panel, k3, p1, k3, p6, k3, p1, [p1, k1] 5 (8, 11, 14) times.
Cont in established patt until piece measures 36 (37, 38, 39) cm (14¼ [14½, 15, 15¼]") from cast on, ending with a WS row.
Place locking m at end of last row to mark beg of armhole.

Shape cap sleeve and front neck
Row 1 (RS) Work 10 (16, 22, 28) sts in Moss st, M1, work in patt to last 2 sts, work 2 tog – 60 (66, 72, 78) sts.
Rows 2–4 Work 3 rows straight, working new st in Moss st.
Row 5 Work 11 (17, 23, 29) sts in Moss st, M1, work in patt to last 2 sts, work 2 tog – 60 (66, 72, 78) sts.
Rows 6–8 Work 3 rows straight.
Row 9 Work 12 (18, 24, 30) sts in Moss st, M1, work in patt to last 2 sts, work 2 tog – 60 (66, 72, 78) sts.
Rows 10–12 Work 3 rows straight.

Rep inc at beg and dec at end of next row, then every 4 rows 8 more times – 60 (66, 72, 78) sts.
Cont dec 1 st at neck edge every 4 rows 2 (3, 4, 5) more times and AT THE SAME TIME shape side edge as foll:
Work 5 rows straight.

Shape upper sleeve and shoulder
Cast off at beg of RS rows 4 sts 7 (8, 9, 10) times, 10 (11, 12, 13) sts once, then 10 sts 2 times.

RIGHT FRONT

Using 3.25 mm (U.S. size 3) needles, cast on 59 (65, 71, 77) sts.
Row 1 (RS) P1, [k1tbl, p1] twice, *k6, p1, [k1tbl, p1] 5 times; rep from * once more, k6, [p1, k1tbl] 7 (10, 13, 16) times.
Row 2 [P1, k1] 7 (10, 13, 16) times, *p6, k1, [p1, k1] 5 times; rep from * once more, p6, [k1, p1] twice, k1.
Row 3 P1, [k1tbl, p1] twice, *C6B, p1, [k1tbl, p1] 5 times; rep from * once more, C6B, [p1, k1tbl] 7 (10, 13, 16) times.
Row 4 Rep Row 2.
Rows 5–32 Rep Rows 1–4 seven more times.
Row 33 P1, [k1tbl, p1] twice, k6, p1, [k1tbl, p1] 5 times, k3, M1, k3, p1, [k1tbl, p1], k6, [p1, k1tbl] 7 (10, 13, 16) times – 60 (66, 72, 78) sts.
Row 34 [P1, k1] 7 (10, 13, 16) times, p6, k1, [p1, k1] 5 times, p7, k1, [p1, k1] 5 times, p6, [k1, p1] 7 times.
Change to 4 mm (U.S. size 6) needles.
Work in patt as foll:
Row 1 (RS) P1, k1tbl, p3, C6B, p3, k1tbl, p3, work Row 19 of Cable Panel, p3, k1tbl, p3, C6B, p3, k1tbl, [p1, k1] 5 (8, 11, 14) times.
Row 2 [K1, p1] 5 (8, 11, 14) times, p1, k3, p6, k3, p1, k3, work Row 20 of Cable Panel, k3, p1, k3, p6, k3, p1, k1.
Row 3 P1, k1tbl, p3, k6, p3, k1tbl, p3, work Row 1 of Cable Panel p3, k1tbl, p3, k6, p3, k1tbl, [p1, k1] 5 (8, 11, 14) times.
Row 4 [K1, p1] 5 (8, 11, 14) times, [p1, k3, p6, k3, p1, k3, work Row 2 of Cable Panel, k3] 3 times, p1, k3, p6, k3, p1, k1.
Cont in established patt until piece measures 36 (37, 38, 39) cm (14¼ [14½, 15, 15¼]") from cast on, ending with a WS row.
Place locking m at beg of last row to mark beg of armhole.

Shape cap sleeves
Row 1 (RS) Work 2 tog, work in patt to last 10 (16, 22, 28) sts, M1, work Moss st to end – 60 (66, 72, 78) sts.
Rows 2–4 Work 3 rows straight, working new st in Moss st.
Row 5 Work 2 tog, work in patt to last 11 (17, 23, 29) sts, M1, work Moss st to end – 60 (66, 72, 78) sts.
Rows 6–8 Work 3 rows straight.
Row 9 Work 2 tog, work in patt to last 12 (18, 24, 30) sts, M1, work Moss st to end – 60 (66, 72, 78) sts.
Rows 10–12 Work 3 rows straight.
Rep dec at beg and inc at end of next row, then every 4 rows 8 more times – 60 (66, 72, 78) sts.
Cont dec 1 st at neck edge every 4 rows 2 (3, 4, 5) times and AT THE SAME TIME shape side edge as foll:
Work 6 rows straight.

Shape upper sleeve and shoulder
Cast off at beg of WS rows 4 sts 7 (8, 9, 10) times, 10 (11, 12, 13) sts once, then 10 sts 2 times.

COLLAR

Using 3.25 mm (U.S. size 3) needles, cast on 187 (195, 203, 211) sts.

Row 1 (RS) [K1tbl, p1] 7 (9, 11, 13) times, *k6, p1, [k1tbl, p1] 5 times; rep from * 5 times, k6, [p1, k1tbl] 7 (9, 11, 13) times.

Row 2 [P1, k1] 7 (9, 11, 13) times, *p6, k1, [p1, k1] 5 times; rep from * 5 times, p6, [k1, p1] 7 (9, 11, 13) times.

Row 3 [K1tbl, p1] 7 (9, 11, 13) times, *C6B, p1, [k1tbl, p1] 5 times; rep from * 8 more times, C6B, [p1, k1tbl] 7 (9, 11, 13) times.

Row 4 Rep Row 2.

Rows 5–8 Rep Rows 1–4 once more.

Shape neck edge

Cast off 3 sts at beg of next 2 rows, then 2 sts at beg on next 2 rows – 177 (185, 193, 201) sts rem.

Rep the last 4 rows 13 more times – 47 (55, 63, 71) sts rem.

Cast off rem sts.

BUTTON BAND

With RS facing and using 3.25 mm (U.S. size 3) needles, start at beg of neck shaping and pick up and k75 (77, 81, 83) sts along left front to bottom edge.

Row 1 (RS) K1tbl, [p1, k1tbl] to end.

Row 2 P1, [k1, p1] to end.

Rep the last 2 rows 3 times more.

Cast off in rib.

BUTTONHOLE BAND

With RS facing and using 3.25 mm (U.S. size 3) needles, start at bottom edge and pick up and k75 (77, 81, 83) sts, along right front edge to beg of neck shaping.

Row 1 (RS) K1tbl, [p1, k1tbl] to end.

Row 2 P1, [k1, p1] to end.

Work 1 more row.

Buttonhole row Work 4 (5, 4, 5) sts in rib, work 2 tog, (yrn) twice, work 2 tog, [work 12 (12, 13, 13) sts in rib, work 2 tog, (yrn) twice, work 2 tog] 4 times, work to end.

Work 4 rows straight.

Cast off in rib.

ARMBANDS

Sew shoulder and upper sleeve seams.

With right side facing and using 3.25 mm (U.S. size 3) needles, pick up and k92 (96, 100, 104) sts between m.

Row 1 (RS) P1, [k1tbl, p1] 4 (5, 6, 7) times, *k6, p1, [k1tbl, p1] 5 times; rep from * 3 more times, k6, [p1, k1tbl] 4 (5, 6, 7) times, p1.

Row 2 K1, [p1, k1] 4 (5, 6, 7) times, *p6, k1, [p1, k1] 5 times; rep from * 3 more times, p6, [k1, p1] 4 (5, 6, 7) times, k1.

Row 3 P1, [k1tbl, p1] 4 (5, 6, 7) times, *C6B, p1, [k1tbl, p1] 5 times; rep from * 3 more times, C6B, [p1, k1tbl] 4 (5, 6, 7) times, p1.

Row 4 Rep Row 2.

Rows 5–8 Rep Rows 1–4 once more.

Cast off in patt, working k2tog over each cable.

MAKING UP

Weave in ends. Block to finished measurements.

Beg and ending at beg of neck shaping, sew cast-off edges of collar to neck edge. Sew ends of front bands to ends of collar. Sew side seams. Sew on buttons.

Cromarty coat

This elegant and interesting triangular shaped coat, knitted in Rowan 'Felted Tweed DK', has a terrific Celtic-inspired pattern on the front panels. You can belt it to add some variety with the shape, giving it an elegant fishtail back.

FINISHED SIZE

To fit bust

81.5	86.5	91.5	96.5	101.5	106.5	112	117	cm
32	34	36	38	40	42	44	46	"

ACTUAL MEASUREMENTS

Bust

96.5	101.5	106.5	112	117	122	127	134	cm
38	40	42	44	46	48	50	52¾	"

Length from front band over shoulders to back neck

56	57	58	59	60	61	62	63	cm
22	22½	22¾	23¼	23½	24	24½	24¾	"

Sleeve length 45 cm (17¾")

YARN

Rowan 'Felted Tweed DK' (50% merino wool, 25% alpaca, 25% viscose; 175 m [191 yd]/50 g):
7 (8, 8, 9, 10, 10, 11, 12) balls in Phantom 153 (A)
2 balls in Scree 165 (B)
1 (1, 1, 1, 2, 2, 2, 2) ball(s) in Clay 177 (C)

NEEDLES

3.25 mm (U.S. size 3) needles: straight and 100 cm (40") long circular
3.75 mm (U.S. size 5) needles: straight and 100 cm (40") long circular. Adjust needle size if necessary to obtain correct tension.

TENSION

23 sts and 30 rows = 10 cm (4") in St st using 3.75 mm (U.S. size 5) needles.
25 sts and 28 rows = 10 cm (4") in colour patt using 3.75 mm (U.S. size 5) needles.

ABBREVIATIONS

See page 150.

BACK AND FRONTS (worked from side to side in one piece starting at right front)
Using 3.25 mm (U.S. size 3) straight needles and A, cast on 99 (102, 105, 108, 111, 114, 117, 120) sts.

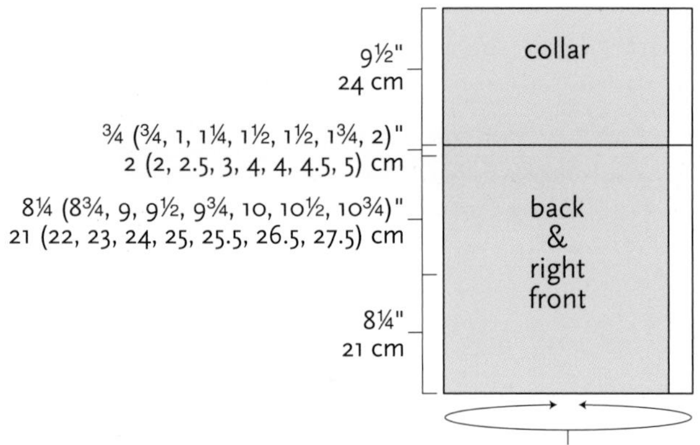

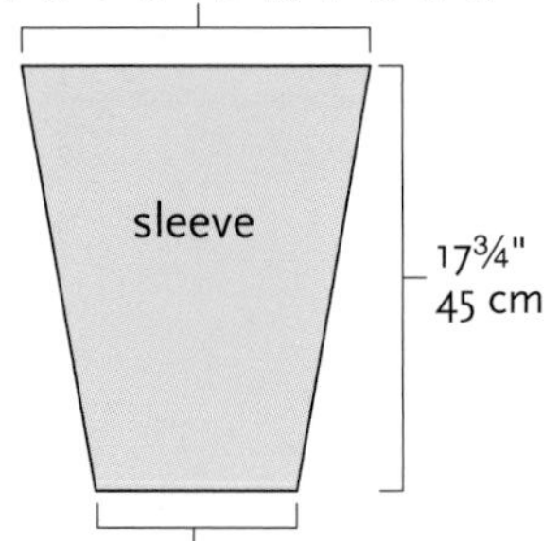

Knit 3 rows.
Change to 3.75 mm (U.S. size 5) needles.
Next row (RS) Knit.
Next row K3, purl to end.
Rep the last 2 rows until piece measures 44 (45, 45.5, 47, 48.5, 49, 50, 51) cm (17¼ [17¾, 18, 18½, 19, 19¼, 19¾, 20]") from cast-on edge, ending with a WS row.

Armhole opening
Next row K4 (5, 6, 7, 8, 9, 10, 11), cast off loosely 48 (50, 52, 54, 56, 58, 60, 62) sts, knit to end – 51 (52, 53, 54, 55, 56, 57, 58) sts rem.
Next row K3, p44, cast on 48 (50, 52, 54, 56, 58, 60, 62) sts over armhole gap, purl to end – 99 (102, 105, 108, 111, 114, 117, 120) sts.
Cont in established patt for 48.5 (51, 53.5, 56, 59, 62, 64, 67.5) cm (19 [20, 21, 22, 23¼, 24½, 25¼, 26½]"), ending with a WS row.

Armhole opening
Next row K4 (5, 6, 7, 8, 9, 10, 11), cast off loosely 48 (50, 52, 54, 56, 58, 60, 62) sts, knit to end – 51 (52, 53, 54, 55, 56, 57, 58) sts rem.
Next row K3, p44, cast on 48 (50, 52, 54, 56, 58, 60, 62) sts, over armhole gap, purl to end – 99 (102, 105, 108, 111, 114, 117, 120) sts.
Cont in established patt for 43 (44, 44.5, 46, 47.5, 48, 49, 50) cm (17 [17¼, 17½, 18, 18¾, 19, 19¼, 19¾]"), ending with a RS row.
Change to 3.25 mm (U.S. size 3) straight needles.
Knit 3 rows.
Cast off all sts.

SLEEVES

Using 3.25 mm (U.S. size 3) straight needles and A, cast on 70 (74, 78, 82, 86, 90, 94, 98) sts.
Rib row 1 (RS) K2, [p2, k2] to end.
Rib row 2 P2, [k2, p2] to end.

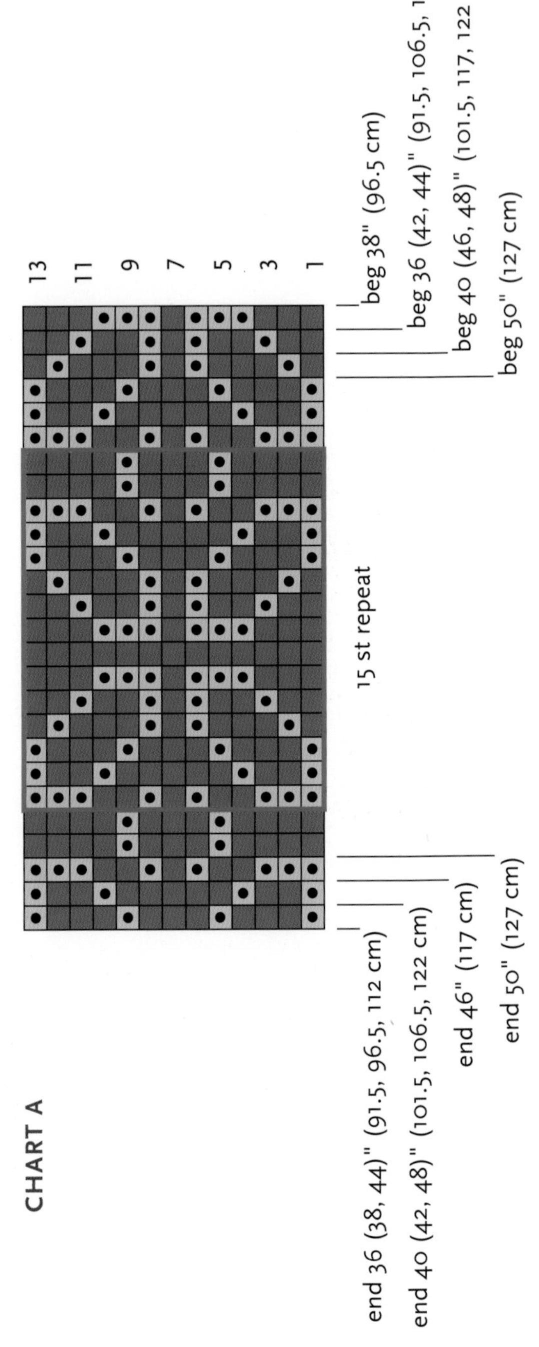

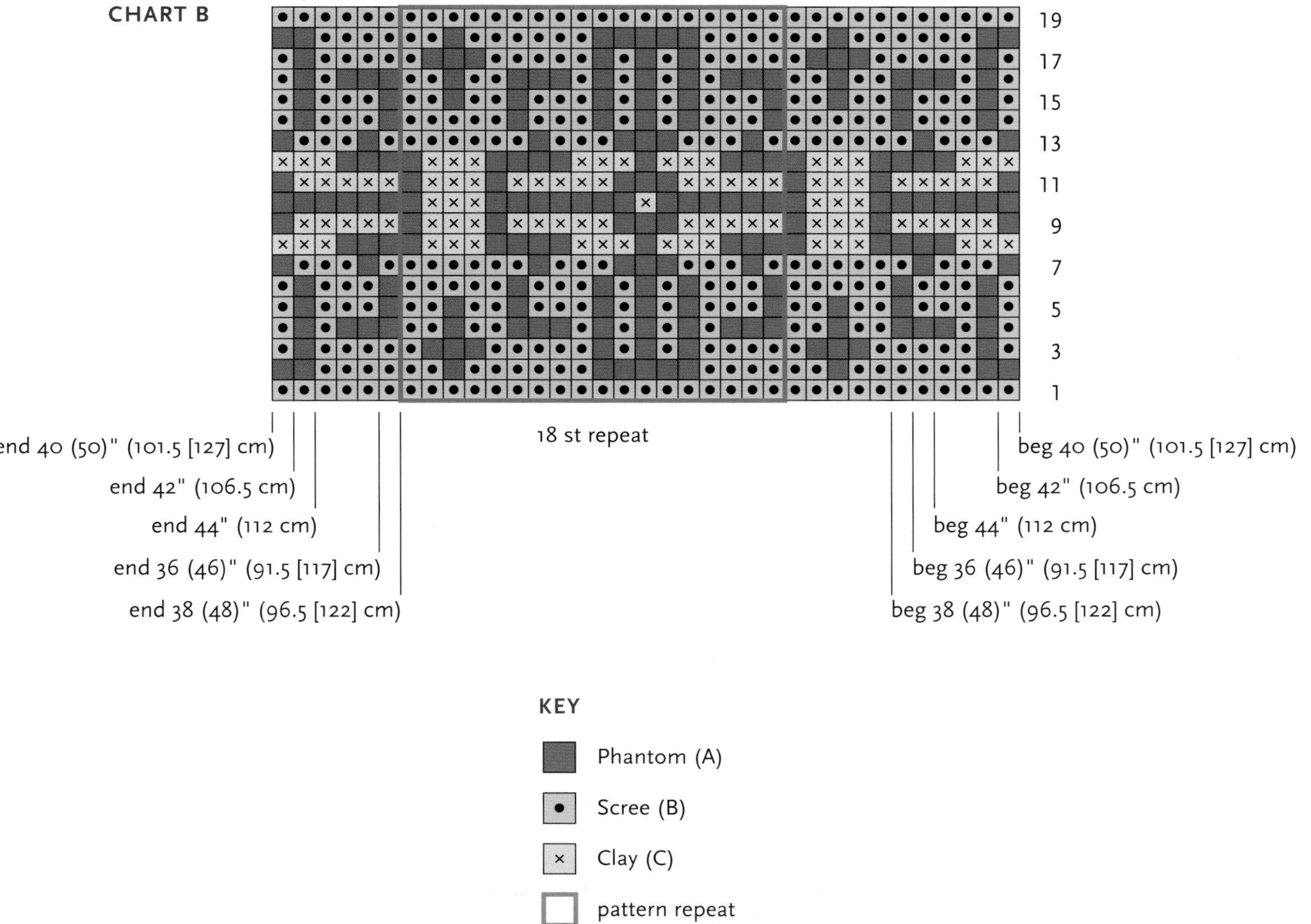
CHART B
19
17
15
13
11
9
7
5
3
1
end 40 (50)" (101.5 [127] cm)
end 42" (106.5 cm)
end 44" (112 cm)
end 36 (46)" (91.5 [117] cm)
end 38 (48)" (96.5 [122] cm)
18 st repeat
beg 40 (50)" (101.5 [127] cm)
beg 42" (106.5 cm)
beg 44" (112 cm)
beg 36 (46)" (91.5 [117] cm)
beg 38 (48)" (96.5 [122] cm)
KEY
Phantom (A)
Scree (B)
Clay (C)
pattern repeat

Rep last 2 rows 6 more times.
Change to 3.75 mm (U.S. size 5) straight needles.
Work 4 rows in established rib patt.
Row 1 (RS) K2, M1, work in established rib patt to last 2 sts, M1, k2 – 2 sts inc'd.
Rows 2 and 4 P3, [k2, p2] to last st, p1.
Row 3 K3 [p2, k3] to last st, k1.
Row 5 (RS) K2, M1, k1, work in established rib patt to last 3 sts, k1, M1, k2 – 2 sts inc'd.
Rows 6 and 8 P4, [k2, p2] to last 2 sts, p2.
Row 7 K4, [p2, k2] to last 2 sts, k2.
Row 9 (RS) K2, M1, work in established rib patt to last 4 sts, k2, M1, k2 – 2 sts inc'd.
Rows 10 and 12 P2, k1, p2, [k2, p2] to last 3 sts, k1, p2.
Row 11 K2, p1, k2, [p2, k2] to last 3 sts, p1, k2.
Row 13 (RS) K2, M1, p1, work in established rib patt to last 3 sts, p1, M1, k2 – 2 sts inc'd.
Rows 14 and 16 P2, [k2, p2] to end.
Row 15 K2, [p2, k2] to end.
Rep Rows 1–16 five more times, then rep Rows 1–5 once more – 122 (126, 130, 134, 138, 142, 146, 150) sts.
Work straight until sleeve measures 45 cm (17¾") from cast-on edge, ending with a WS row.
Cast off.

FRONT BAND

Using 3.75 mm (U.S. size 5) circular needle and A, cast on 391 (407, 419, 435, 451, 463, 479, 491) sts.
Row 1 K3, purl to last 3 sts, k3.
Beg with a RS row, work in St st and patt from Chart A as foll:
Row 1 Knit 3A, work 5 (6, 4, 5, 5, 4, 4, 3) sts before rep, work 15-st rep of Row 1 of Chart A 25 (26, 27, 28, 29, 30, 31, 32) times, work 5 (5, 4, 4, 5, 3, 4, 2) sts after rep, knit 3A.
Row 2 Knit 3A, work 5 (5, 4, 4, 5, 3, 4, 2) sts before rep, work 15-st rep of Row 2 of Chart A 25 (26, 27, 28, 29, 30, 31, 32) times, work 5 (6, 4, 5, 5, 4, 4, 3) sts after rep, knit 3A.
Rows 3–13 Cont in established patt to end of chart Row 13.
Row 14 Using A, k3, purl to last 3 sts, k3.
Row 15 Using A, knit.
Row 16 Knit 3A, [purl 2C, 2A] to last 4 sts, purl 1C, knit 3A.
Row 17 Knit 5A, [2C, 2A] to last 6 sts, knit 2C, 4A.
Row 18 Knit 3A, [purl 2A, 2C] to last 4 sts, purl 1A, knit 3A.
Row 19 Knit 3A, [2C, 2A] to last 4 sts, 1C, 3A.
Rows 20 and 21 Rep Rows 14 and 15.
Beg with a WS row, work in St st and patt from Chart B as foll:
Row 22 Knit 3A, work 1 (0, 6, 5, 4, 1, 0, 6) st(s) before rep, work 18-st rep of Row 1 of Chart B 21 (22, 22, 23, 24, 25, 26, 26) times, work 6 (5, 11, 10, 9, 6, 5, 11) sts after rep, knit 3A.
Row 23 Knit 3A, work 6 (5, 11, 10, 9, 6, 5, 11) sts before rep, work 18-st rep of Row 2 of Chart B 21 (22, 22, 23, 24, 25, 26, 26) times, work 1 (0, 6, 5, 4, 1, 0, 6) st(s) after rep, knit 3A.
Rows 24–40 Cont in established patt to end of chart Row 19.
Row 41 Using A, knit.
Row 42 Using A, k3, purl to last 3 sts, k3.
Rows 43–46 Rep Rows 16–19.
Rows 47 and 48 Rep Rows 41 and 42.
Rows 49–61 Rep Rows 1–13.
Change to 3.25 mm (U.S. size 3) circular needle.
Using A, knit 3 rows.
Cast off.

MAKING UP

Sew sleeve seams. Sew in sleeves. Sew on front edging, easing front edging to fit.

Orkney throw

This elegant throw, knitted in Rowan 'Pure Wool Aran', is created from large alternating rectangular patches of a geometric textured pattern and moss stitch. The pieces are reversible, so you can choose which side you use, as the raised seams have an interesting texture of their own.

FINISHED SIZE
171.5 x 169 cm (67½ x 66½")

YARN
26 balls of Rowan 'Pure Wool Aran' (100% superwash wool; 170 m [186 yd]/100 g) in Tough 696

NEEDLES
Pair of 4.5 mm (U.S. size 7) knitting needles
Adjust needle size if necessary to obtain correct tension.

TENSION
Each block measures 34.5 x 24 cm (13½ x 9½").

ABBREVIATIONS
See page 150.

NOTE

Read Chart from right to left on RS rows and from left to right on WS rows.

BLOCK A (make 18)

Using 4.5 mm (U.S. size 7) needles, cast on 65 sts.
Work in patt from Block A chart to end of row 64.
Cast off.

BLOCK B (make 17)

Using 4.5 mm (U.S. size 7) needles, cast on 65 sts.
Moss st row K1, [p1, k1] to end.
Rep the last row 79 times.
Cast off.

MAKING UP

With a Block A in each corner, sew blocks together alternating Blocks A and B to form a rectangle 5 blocks wide by 7 blocks long, using photo as guide.

ASSEMBLY DIAGRAM

A	B	A	B	A
B	A	B	A	B
A	B	A	B	A
B	A	B	A	B
A	B	A	B	A
B	A	B	A	B
A	B	A	B	A

BLOCK A CHART

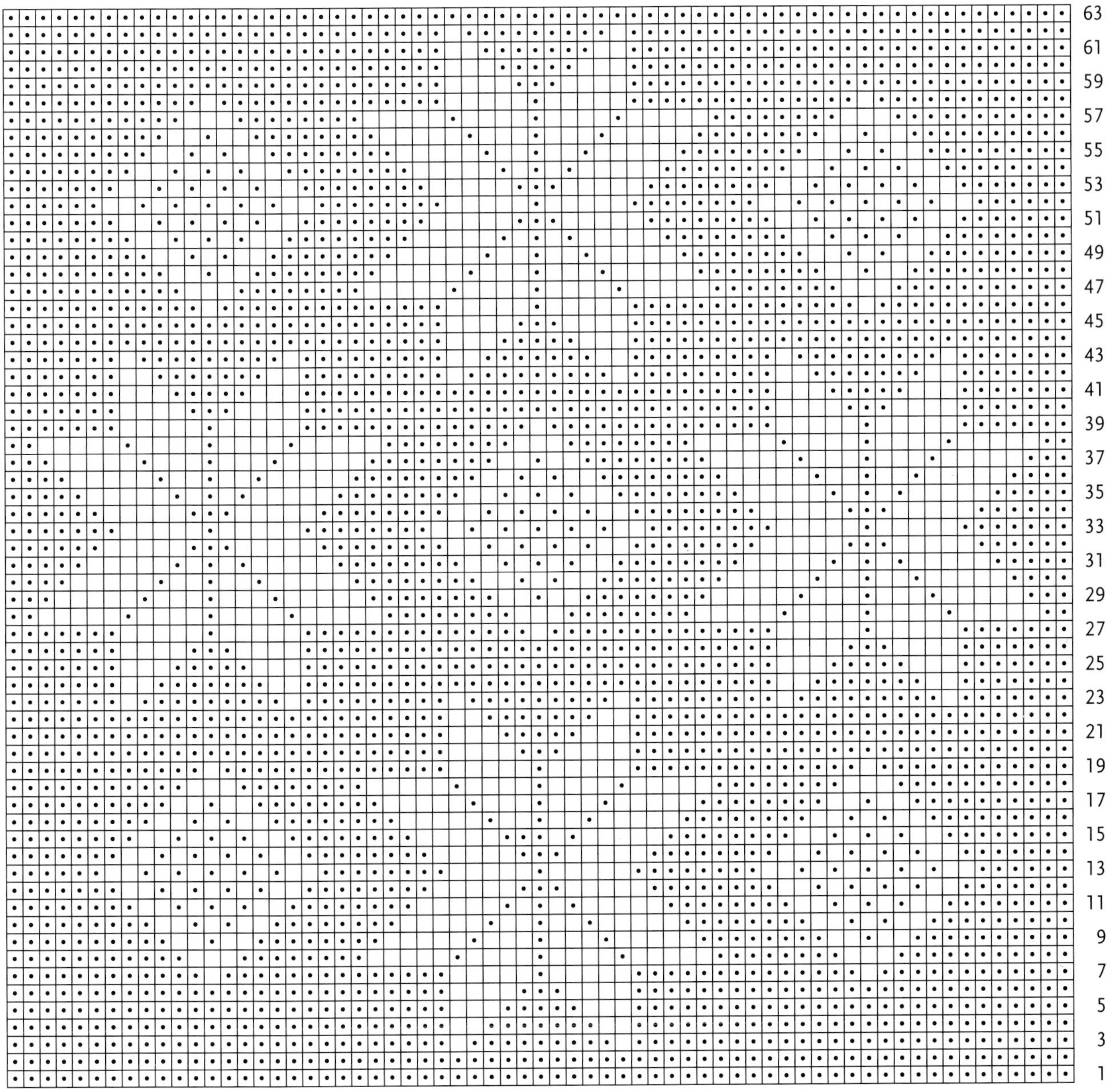

65 sts

KEY

- ☐ k on RS, p on WS
- ⊡ p on RS, k on WS

Knitting know-how

SIZING

The instructions are given for the smallest size, and larger sizes follow in parentheses. If there is only one set of figures, it refers to all sizes. If - (hyphen) or 0 (zero) is given in an instruction for the size you are knitting, then that particular instruction does not apply to your size.

Included with each garment pattern in this book is a size diagram of the finished garment pieces and their dimensions. The size diagram shows the finished width of the garment at the underarm point, and it is this measurement that you should choose first; a useful tip is to measure one of your own garments that is a comfortable fit. Having chosen a size based on width, look at the corresponding length for that size; if you are not happy with the total recommended length, adjust your own garment before beginning your armhole shaping – any adjustment after this point will mean that your sleeve will not fit into your garment easily. Don't forget to take your adjustment into account if there is any side-seam shaping.

TENSION

Obtaining the correct tension can make the difference between a successful garment and a disastrous one. It controls both the shape and size of an article, so any variation, however slight, can distort the finished garment.

You must match the tension given at the start of each pattern. To check your tension, knit a square in the pattern stitch and/or stocking stitch of perhaps 5–10 more stitches and 5–10 more rows than those given in the tension note. Press the finished square under a damp cloth and mark out the central 10 cm (4") square with pins. If you have too many stitches to 10 cm (4"), try again using thicker needles. If you have too few stitches to 10 cm (4"), try again using finer needles. Once you have achieved the correct tension, your garment will be knitted to the measurements shown in the size diagram with the pattern.

CABLE PATTERNS

Cable stitch patterns allow you to twist the stitches in various ways, to create decorative effects such as an interesting rope-like structure to the knitting. The cables can be thin and fine (just a couple of stitches wide) or really big and chunky (up to 8 stitches or more).

To work cables, you need to hold the appropriate number of stitches that form the cable twist (abbreviated in pattern as C) on a separate small cable needle, while you knit behind or in front of them. You then knit the stitches off the cable needle before continuing to knit the remaining stitches in the row. Depending on whether the cable needle is at the front or the back of the work, the cables will twist to the left or right but the principle remains the same. A four-stitch cable will be abbreviated as C4F or C4B depending on whether the cable needle is held to the front or back of the work.

Colourwork

There are two main methods of working with colour in knitted fabrics: the intarsia and the

Fairisle techniques. The first method produces a single thickness of fabric and is usually used where a new colour is required for a block of stitches and rows in a particular area of a piece of knitting. Where a small repeating colour pattern of up to 3 or 4 stitches is created across the row, the Fairisle technique is generally used.

INTARSIA

In the intarsia technique, you have to join in a new yarn colour for each new block of colour stitches. To prevent the yarns getting twisted on the ball, the simplest method is to make individual little balls of yarn, or bobbins, from pre-cut short lengths of yarn, one for each motif or block of colour used in a row. You then work across the stitches, joining in the colours as required, by twisting them around each other where they meet on the wrong side of the work, to avoid gaps. After you have completed the piece of knitting, you need to neaten up the loose ends. They can either be woven in along the colour joins or they can be knitted in to the fabric as each colour is worked by picking up the loops of the yarns carried across the back of the work as you knit.

FAIRISLE

When you are working a pattern with two or more repeating colours in the same row, you need to strand the yarn not in use behind the stitches being worked. Do this with care, loosely enough to ensure that the strands not in use do not tighten and pucker the front of the knitting. Treat the yarns not in use, known as 'floating yarns', as if they were one yarn and spread the stitches as you work to their correct width to keep them elastic. If your pattern demands that the stranded or floating yarns are carried across more than three stitches, it is wise to weave the new yarn colour under and over the colour yarn you are working with each time you change colours (over the first time, under the second time, and so on). The alternating 'under and over' movement prevents the floating yarns from tangling by keeping them caught at the back of the work. It is important when knitting with more than one colour to keep your tension correct, as it easy to pull the loops of yarn too tight, puckering the work. If you tend to knit colourwork too tightly, increase your needle size for the colourwork section.

Finishing methods

PRESSING

Block out each piece of knitting by pinning it on a board to the correct measurements in the pattern. Then lightly press it according to the ball band instructions, omitting any ribbed areas. Take special care to press the edges as this makes sewing up easier and neater. If you cannot press the fabric, then cover the knitted fabric with a damp cloth and leave to stand for a couple of hours. Weave in all ends neatly along the selvedge edge or a colour join, as appropriate.

STITCHING SEAMS

When you stitch the pieces together, remember to match any areas of colour and texture carefully where they meet. Use a special seam stitch, called mattress stitch (in which you pick up a small stitch from the edge of each seam to be joined), as it creates the flattest seam. After all the seams are complete, press the seams and hems. Lastly, sew on any buttons to correspond with the positions of any buttonholes.

Abbreviations

The knitting pattern abbreviations used in this book are as below:

alt	alternate
approx	approximate
beg	begin(s)(ning)
cm	centimetres
cont	continu(e)(ing)
dec	decreas(e)(ing)
foll	follow(s)(ing)
garter st	garter stitch (K every row)
in	inch(es)
inc	increas(e)(ing)
K	knit
kfb	knit in front and back of same stitch
K2tog	knit next 2 sts together
m	metre(s)
M1	make one st by picking up horizontal loop before next st and knitting into back of it
mm	millimetres
P	purl
patt	pattern
pfb	purl in front and back of same stitch
psso	pass slipped stitch over
p2sso	pass two slipped stitches over
P2tog	purl next 2 sts together
rem	remain(s)(ing)
rep	repeat
rev St st	reverse stocking stitch
RS	right side
skp	sl 1, k1, psso
sl 1	slip one stitch
ssk	slip, slip, knit
st(s)	stitch(es)
St st	stocking stitch (1 row K, 1 row P)
tbl	through back of loop(s)
tog	together
WS	wrong side
wyib	with yarn held at back
wyif	with yarn held at front
yd	yard(s)
yf	yarn forward
yrn	yarn round needle

Rowan yarns

The yarns used in this book are all Rowan yarns. Their specifications are given here. If you use a substitute yarn, take care to match the required tension by doing a test swatch of the chosen substitution and changing needle size as necessary.

Felted Tweed DK
A wool-alpaca-viscose mix; 50 per cent merino wool, 25 per cent alpaca, 25 per cent viscose; 50 g/1¾ oz (approx 175 m/191 yd) per ball. Recommended tension: 22–24 sts and 30–32 rows to 10 cm (4") using 3.5–4 mm (U.S. size 5–6) knitting needles.

Felted Tweed Aran
An aran weight merino wool-alpaca-viscose mix yarn; 50 per cent merino wool, 25 per cent alpaca, 15 per cent viscose; 50 g/1¾ oz (87 m/95 yd) per ball. Recommended tension: 16 sts and 23 rows to 10 cm (4") measured over St st using 5 mm (U.S. size 8) knitting needles.

Rowan Fine Tweed
A 100 per cent pure wool; 25 g /⅞ oz (approx 90 m/98 yd) per ball. Recommended tension: 26½ sts and 38 rows to 10 cm (4") using 3.25 mm (U.S. size 3) knitting needles.

Rowan Tweed
A 100 per cent pure wool DK weight yarn; 50 g/1¾ oz (approx 118 m/129 yd) per ball. Recommended tension: 21 sts and 30 rows to 10 cm (4") using 4 mm (U.S. size 6) needles.

Rowan Tweed Aran
A 100 per cent pure wool Aran weight yarn; 50 g/1¾ oz (approx 96 m/105 yd) per ball. Recommended tension: 17–19 sts and 23–25 rows to 10 cm (4") using 4.5–5 mm (U.S. size 7–8) needles.

Pure Wool Aran
An Aran weight 100 per cent pure superwash wool yarn; 100 g/3½ oz (approx 170 m/186 yd) per ball. Recommended tension: 17–19 sts and 23–25 rows to 10 cm (4") using 4.5–5 mm (U.S. size 7–8) knitting needles.

Stockists

U.K.
Rowan, Green Lane Mill, Holmfirth,
West Yorkshire, HD9 2DX
Tel: +44 (0) 1484 681881
www.knitrowan.com

U.S.A.
Westminster Fibers Inc,
Nashua, NH 03060
Tel: (800) 445-9276
www.westminsterfibers.com

AUSTRALIA
Australian Country Spinners Pty Ltd,
Melbourne 3004
Tel: 03 9380 3830
Email: tkohut@auspinners.com.au

BENELUX
Coats Benelux, Ninove, 9400
Tel: 00 32 54 318989
Email: sales.coatsninove@coats.com

CANADA
See U.S.A.

CHINA
Coats Shanghai Ltd, Shanghai
Tel: 86 21 5774 3733
Email: victor.li@coats.com

DENMARK
Coats HP A/S, Copenhagen
Tel: 45 35 86 90 49
www.coatscrafts.dk

FINLAND
Coats Opti Crafts Oy, Kerava, 04220
Tel: (358) 9 274871
wwwcoatscrafts.fi

FRANCE
Coats Steiner, Mehun-Sur-Yèvre,
18500
Tel: 02 48 23 12 30
www.coatscrafts.fr

GERMANY
Coats GmbH, Kenzingen, 79341
Tel: 07162-14346
www.coatsgmbh.de

HONG KONG
See China

ICELAND
Rowan At Storkurinn, Reykjavik, 101
Tel: 551 8258
www.storkurinn.is

ISRAEL
Beit Hasidkit, Kfar Sava, 44256
Tel: (972) 9 7482381

ITALY
Coats Cucirini srl, Milano, 20126
Tel: (02) 636151
www.coatscucirini.com

KOREA
Coats Korea Co. Lt, Seoul, 137-060
Tel: 82-2-521-6262
www.coatskorea.co.kr

NEW ZEALAND
ACS New Zealand, Christchurch
Tel: 64-3-323-6665

NORWAY
Coats Knappehuset AS, Bergen,
5873
Tel: 55 53 93 00

PORTUGAL
Coats & Clark, Vila Nova de Gaia
4431-968
Tel: 223770700
www.crafts.com.pt

SINGAPORE
Golden Dragon Store, Singapore
Tel: (65) 65358454/65358234
Email: gdscraft@hotmail.com

SOUTH AFRICA
Arthur Bales Ltd, Johannesburg,
2195
Tel: (27) 118 882 401
www.arthurbales.co.za

SPAIN
Coats Fabra, Barcelona, 08030
Tel: (34) 93 290 84 00
www.coatscrafts.es

SWEDEN
Coats Expotex AB, Goteborg, 431 30
Tel: (46) 33 720 79 00
www.coatscrafts.se

SWITZERLAND
Coats Stroppel AG, Turgi (AG),
CH-5300
Tel: 056 298 12 20
www.coatscrafts.ch

TAIWAN
Cactus Quality Co Ltd, Taiwan,
R.O.C. 10084
Tel: 00886-2-23656527
www.excelcraft.com.tw

For stockists in all other countries
please contact Rowan for details

Acknowledgements

PUBLISHERS' ACKNOWLEDGEMENTS
The publishers would like to thank Anne Wilson for the layouts, John Heseltine for model photography (and Ed Berry, Steve Wooster and Hazel Young for additional photography), Katie Hardwicke for editing, Penny Hill for pattern writing and knitting, Therese Chynoweth for charts and pattern checking, Tessa (Storm), Daisy (Nevs), Stephanie Edgar and Holly Walker for modelling, JJ locations for the interior location and the Barn Theatre, Welwyn, for its studio location.

AUTHOR'S ACKNOWLEDGEMENTS
Martin Storey would like to thank Penny Hill and her team of knitters for the beautifully knitted designs featured in this book; Teresa Gogay for her invaluable help on knitting the swatches; and Kate Buller, Marie Wallin and David Macleod at Rowan for their continuous support.